Living Revision

Living Revision

A Writer's Craft as Spiritual Practice

Elizabeth Jarrett Andrew

Skinner House Books
Boston

www.skinnerhouse.org

Printed in the United States

Cover design by Kathryn Sky-Peck
Text design by Suzanne Morgan
Author photo by Jennifer Larson

print ISBN: 978-1-55896-801-1
eBook ISBN: 978-1-55896-802-8

6 5 4 3
25 24 23

Library of Congress Cataloging-in-Publication Data
Names: Andrew, Elizabeth, 1969- author.
Title: Living revision : a writer's craft as spiritual practice / Elizabeth
   Jarrett Andrew.
Description: Boston : Skinner House Books, 2017. | Includes bibliographical
   references.
Identifiers: LCCN 2017010417 (print) | LCCN 2017028483 (ebook) | ISBN
   9781558968028 | ISBN 9781558968011 (pbk. : alk. paper)
Subjects: LCSH: Authorship--Philosophy.
Classification: LCC PN175 (ebook) | LCC PN175 .A53 2017 (print) | DDC
   801--dc23
LC record available at https://lccn.loc.gov/2017010417

Sometimes the words are so close I am
more who I am when I'm down on paper
than anywhere else as if my life were
practicing for the real me I become
unbuttoned from the anecdotal and
unnecessary and undressed down
to the figure of the poem, line by line,
the real text a child could understand.
Why do I get confused living it through?
Those of you, lost and yearning to be free,
who hear these words, take heart from me.
I once was in as many drafts as you.
But briefly, essentially, here I am . . .
Who touches this poem touches a woman.

Julia Alvarez

Contents

Toolboxes

Foreword

Dear Reader,

As I write to you now, I'm sitting in my attic loft, gazing out the window where I see children walking their familiar paths to school. I witness this scene every weekday morning, if I arrive early enough at my desk. The children all carry backpacks affixed to their small bodies. Some swing on their parents' hands, while others skip ahead, absorbed in conversation with one another. Despite their different approaches, the children all seem eager to get to the playground and allow the new day to commence.

I have been a writer for more than thirty years. And always, I *want* to feel like that child skipping to school—knowing where I'm going and eager to participate in what will happen when I get there. But, alas, writing is not so straightforward. Often, I avoid this very task to which I've devoted my life. Why?

Perhaps it's because writing, if done well, asks so much of us. It demands that we be authentic to ourselves and to our readers. Writing asks that we not only dig out the essential material—sifting to separate the good stuff from the dreck—but also that we keep honing and refining our words until they articulate a story, an idea, or a meaning that goes beyond ourselves. It's hard work that often feels as though it's carried out in solitary confinement.

Thank goodness, then, for the allies who come along just when we need them most. And if we're smart, we crack open the door and let them in. Luckily, right now you're holding the hand of a superb writing friend—Elizabeth Jarrett Andrew, in the form of her book *Living Revision*. She will lead you, gently, into the territory many of us fear the most: the land of revision, where what was just a glimmer must now morph into our true writing.

I've often told my students that revision is an "acquired taste." They never believe me. They want to have the full story or poem arrive full-blown on the page, to be done with it mere minutes after conception. But, I tell them, those first drafts, those attempts, are merely creating the raw material; once you have the substance to play with (I often call it "playdough"), then the *real* work can commence. And this stage of writing can be just as creative as—and perhaps more exhilarating than—the discovery work itself.

In *Living Revision,* Elizabeth Jarrett Andrew articulates both the struggles and the *joy* of revision, in a way that will make you eager to dive back into all phases of writing with renewed vigor. She helps us revise our conceptions of revision itself and shows us how a positive approach to revision can sharpen the core practice of attention essential to any writing endeavor. She describes the page as a living thing, with its own elusive "heartbeat" we need to discover and amplify.

The book builds from there, addressing the emotional, spiritual, and practical aspects of writing and revision. In addition to using examples and wise advice from other writers, Andrew gives us a plethora of astute exercises that provide many ways to think differently and creatively about your work as it grows. I can't wait to share this book with my students, and to use it myself. I'll keep this book in my metaphorical backpack as I walk that familiar path toward my writing desk, eager to see what new delights might await me there.

Brenda Miller
author of *Listening Against the Stone*
co-author of *The Pen and the Bell: Mindful Writing in a Busy World*

Introduction

Writing creatively helps us come alive. The thrill of discovery, of growing in awareness, of forming ideas into language and image and story, of ourselves being formed in the process . . . *this* is why we first began writing, and what prods us to continue. Writing feeds the spirit. How and why this is so remain a mystery, but I'm convinced of it regardless: Writing is one way we humans enter, and invite others to enter, a fully textured, openhearted engagement with life.

How easily we forget this! Too soon, other agendas take over. We want an audience, a stay against mortality, revenge, fame, the comfort of being heard, the MFA degree; we want to record the past, sing praises, make a difference, make Art, make waves, or any number of shifting, contradictory ends. Especially after the first draft is complete, after we've reveled in its brilliance and despaired at its defects, we sense that something more is possible, for ourselves as writers and for our project. Surely this story can be better. Surely we can transform our writing from private ramblings into influential prose, from a record of events into an engaging narrative, from a simple idea to a smart, nuanced exploration. We long for artistic fulfillment—for arrival, which we often equate with publication.

Ask most writers, editors, and agents how to get there and they'll give the same answer: revision. Writing *is* revision, the professionals claim; writing is the gut-wrenching, revelatory, dogged work of developing a story.

Yes, writing is revision. But I'm here to say that revision is not just for the professionals or those wanting an audience. **At its most basic, revision is seeing anew**. Revision is the complicated, profound work of creation—an act that simultaneously creates within and through the creator. Revision changes the writer, deepens the writer's work, and infuses that work with the potential to move readers. Revision addresses our innermost longings. At its core, revision is the spiritual practice of transformation—of seeing text, and therefore the world, with new eyes. Done well, revision returns us to our original love.

Why then does the suggestion of revision make most of us cringe? Revision, we've been taught, means bleeding red ink on the page, "killing our darlings" as William Faulkner so unpleasantly put it, and years of Herculean labor. Revision implies that our first, muse-bestowed inspiration is (don't say it!) flawed. Revision asks us to gamble an initial attempt on the chance of something better.

It's a rare writer whose heart doesn't plummet when faced with revision. Case in point: After plugging away at this book for six years, I got a sudden sparkling insight that reframed everything. In a passion, I rewrote the introduction and sent it off to my writing group for their approval. They slammed on the brakes. Sure, it was a good idea, but what about . . . ? Once again I swallowed my pride, considered their questions, and began again.

How do writers do it? How do I—how does anyone—muster the stamina, the innovation, and the heart to revise? Why bother?

"You can fall in love with your first draft," the poet and memoirist Jorie Miller likes to say, "but don't marry it." We enter mature and lasting relationships with creative work through revision. Like any healthy commitment, revision demands of us practices that commonly make us groan: balancing the joy of spontaneity and inspiration with the efficacy of restraint and discipline. Attaching ourselves wholeheartedly to the work while also holding it lightly. Exercising humility. Listening deeply. Seeking what's true and naming it as best we can. Facing the full range of our humanity, from utterly broken to fabulously beautiful. Being willing to grow. Practicing patience, discernment, compassion. **Revision requires inner work and thus is a spiritual practice**. Through revision's grueling demands and absorbing joys, we come more alive.

Most people don't want to make this effort because they don't realize revision is the work of learning to love. Love isn't just a feeling; it's an act of will, consent, and surrender. Love takes time. Love is what brings us and our writing to fruition.

This book is an introduction to the long-term practice of enlivening yourself and your writing. It will teach you what commitment looks like in the literary world—how to take your head-over-heels romance with an idea through development into maturity. On the surface, much of this book looks like lessons in craft—how to discover your story's structure or develop your themes or use the reflective voice. Literary techniques are essentially tried-and-true methods for engaging the human heart within and across the page. If you want to develop your work, whether for your own sake or for that of an audience, here are the tools you need. This book will help you thrive on the long road to completion. With a new relationship to revision and some tools under your belt, you can manifest the full potential of your project. Anyone can; everyone can.

Look beyond the craft lessons, however, and you'll find here a reliable framework for personal growth. Writers' journeys toward self-discovery and the evolution of their craft are inseparable. Our capacity to transform our writing is intricately connected to our willingness to change how we see our subjects and the world. If you write for personal exploration, here you will find the tools you need to bring discipline and depth to this practice. Revision exercises spiritual muscles. It strengthens our relationship to the creative source.

So take heed: Revision, like love, is not for the fainthearted. **For your writing to change, you must change**. In these pages I won't offer you blithe literary exercises to help you manipulate your text. I'm not interested in aesthetics for aesthetics' sake. I want you to write with spirit and power, to write as though your life is on fire— which it is—and to write to a world thirsty for truth. This book is an invitation to open your heart wide, for the sake of your creation and all creation.

A Note on How to Work with This Book

When monks approached the fourth-century desert monastic Abba Moses to ask him what they needed to know God, Moses said, "Go to your cell and your cell will teach you everything." How can we learn to write? Go to the page; the page will teach you everything.

In this book I quote a lot of wise people, offer helpful ideas, and recommend some fabulous books. Writers need to eat, drink, and breathe books. But the best way to learn to revise is to do it. Do the exercises. Let the page be your teacher.

The first third of this book will revise your ideas about revision. The second and third parts show you how to strengthen your art and open your heart using classic literary techniques in early and late revision. The Toolboxes throughout present basic tools for seeing your work with new eyes. And the exercises help you apply these ideas. Not all the exercises will be relevant to you or to your current project. Do those that inspire you, confound you, or ignite your resistance. If you get bogged down by theory in the first third, skip ahead to a Toolbox or to the second two-thirds. Remember, however, that you may need to fundamentally shift your thinking about revision before it can offer you its gifts.

Please don't assume that because this book distinguishes between early and late revision you need write only two drafts. No magic number of revisions will bring your idea to fruition, but I guarantee it's more than two. Rather than trying to economize with a few packed, multitasking revisions, I suggest tackling one or two craft issues per draft and writing abundant drafts. Focusing will prove faster in the long haul.

A Caveat about Genre

In this book I don't differentiate much between fiction, creative nonfiction, and poetry. The same basic principles of revision apply regardless of genre. When writers stake out and defend their genre turf, they shut down possibilities for their work. This is why I quote freely from poets in a book dedicated to prose writing, and why I rarely make distinctions between fiction and creative nonfiction.

For this reason also I use the word *story* to encompass any creative work with emotional or aesthetic movement. An essay tells a story of ideas. A poem tells the story of a moment or feeling. Stories edit experience, lending it beginning, middle, and end and positing significance. To make a story, we craft a bit of life into meaningful form.

Revising Our Ideas about Revision

CHAPTER ONE

Starting Rough

Initial drafts are an adventure. That first gesture of catching an idea and wrapping it in language is awe inspiring. Mystery draws us forward: Why do I tremble at this memory? What will this character say next? What do I *really* think about this subject? Writers bring to the blank page an idea—some motivating spark—but we don't know its form, we don't know half the content, we often don't know the *real* reason we're writing. We certainly don't yet know which exact sentences will emerge. We come with an agenda but also, ideally, an open heart and a willingness to be surprised.

Beginning writers have the advantage here. Their process is uncharted, their material untapped. The phenomenon that writing changes the writer is astonishing. New writers often seem starstruck; they're head over heels in love with a wisdom that's been hiding in their handwriting.

Most people discover the delight of writing when journaling or playing in a notebook. Such readerless writing has great merit. It teems with discovery. You record a memory of a grandmother's sewing box and are surprised to remember a love letter you once found there. You write down a dream and watch a shockingly lovely phrase appear on the page. You write out your anger at your brother-in-law and find by the end of the entry that your emotion has dissipated. Rough, deeply personal writing like this, writing that rarely sees an audience, acts as a sounding board against which we can hear the workings of our inner being. It inhabits a protected space where we can heed silent proddings, often for the first time.

Readerless writing changes us. When writers—and I refer to everyone who writes as a writer, regardless of whether they publish their work—describe writing as therapeutic or spiritual, usually they've experienced the transformative power of journaling or drafting. They find there delight and insight. They like who they've become for having written. Writing is essential to writers' well-being; it helps us be conscious and attentive. It makes us feel alive.

This is important! Too many writers, as we revise and publish, forget to tend these simple joys. We forget that our love of writing makes it worthwhile. Publication, recognition, and accomplishment are all icing on the cake. If we neglect this love, we lose it, along with the grace that love lends our prose.

Genuine, openhearted engagement—what Brenda Ueland calls "interestingness"—is the basic ingredient of a fruitful creative process. Because of this, stories are essentially egalitarian in nature, meaning that each and every one of us ordinary people who writes has the capacity to move a reader. Have you ever sat through a memorial service at which a grieving grandchild read a coarse but genuine rendering of the departed one's life and set everyone weeping? Have you ever received a card that touched you so profoundly you saved it for years? When I taught seventh grade, my struggling students always floored me with their poetry; it was raw and real because they put their hearts into it and spoke the truth. They didn't yet have the self-consciousness or ambitions that trip most of us up.

Talent and skill and craft and effort will all increase the effectiveness of our writing, but the essential ingredients for stirring a reader's heart are available to everyone who loves writing: curiosity, dedication, and courage. Much of the work of learning to write effectively involves stripping away all that interferes with our natural inclinations to explore, and expanding our capacity to recognize and name the truth.

For this reason I believe that artistic creation is inherently worthy. Writers don't need to finish projects or amass sales figures or achieve literary stature for their work to have value. The process itself is worthy. As Annie Dillard once said, even an unpublished, unread manuscript hiding under a bed in an attic exerts its influence on the world. Creative endeavors have devious, often invisible ways of affecting us, usually for the better.

The good news for those who want to move readers is that "interestingness" is infectious. "The writer has a feeling and utters it from his true self," Brenda Ueland teaches. "The reader reads it and is immediately infected. He has exactly the same feeling. This is the whole secret of enchantment." It's also the secret of revision, and what you and I are going to unpack together.

Toolbox: How to Write a Successful Rough Draft

Write fast. Write to explore. Write with exuberance. Be fearless. Fully invest yourself in discovery, delight, and play. Write for no audience, or write for an infinitely friendly and inviting audience, or consider your audience briefly and then set these considerations aside. Write because it's fun. Write for the love of it.

"A careful first draft," Patricia Hampl warns, "is a failed first draft." Yes, rough drafts can succeed or fail, but not because of the qualities (craft, elegance, wisdom, imagination) we expect. Even Anne Lamott's advice to write a "shitty first draft" is misleading; drafts needn't be sloppy. Success in a draft is determined by the author's full-hearted, honest involvement with the work alongside a carefree relationship to the text. Is the project important to the writer? Then it matters. Are both the words and the writer's heart still malleable? Then both can be shaped. The draft's a success.

There are those who can draft a multifaceted piece on the first go-round: a few lucky geniuses, journalists, and others highly disciplined in conceptualizing an entire project before beginning. But just because a few *can* doesn't mean we all *should*. In art making, evolution is the rule rather than the exception. That most of us aren't brilliant or trained enough to ease our ideas into fine literature on the first try implies nothing about our potential, nor about our work's worth. Draft your work as though it's an essay—an attempt—that will be followed by many more.

Sol Stein recommends that we triage our work, organizing the writing process to address systemic problems first, then working our way down to the minor tweaks. The primary task of a rough draft is to discover what the story might say and why the writer might care. Without these elements—a story, a drive—nothing else can happen. You can't fix a blank page, as Nora Roberts says, and why bother if you don't care?

More to our purposes here, however, the spirit of exploration is best served by understanding the messy ardor of drafting as the start of a long, steady, gentle relationship. Writing through multiple revisions is healthy. It's sustainable. We can learn a lot. With few exceptions, influential literature is made this way. With no exceptions, this is how lasting transformation in writing happens.

What material fires you up, and why? What process gives you the most freedom? What encourages you to experiment? What makes you feel safe enough to be completely honest and vulnerable? What helps you find the story? What *works*? Regardless of writerly advice, mine or others', always follow the work.

Tips for Drafting

- Write for yourself alone. Thoughts of an audience almost always limit early drafts of creative work. If an audience impinges itself on your process, try conceiving of your audience as entirely receptive and welcoming. If an audience inspires or motivates you, cultivate the life-giving qualities of your audience while dismissing those that restrict you.

- Hold everything that lands on the page lightly. For most of us, this is easier to do if we set perfectionism aside. Avoid polish.

- If you prefer to plan ahead, quickly sketch out the story as a rough outline or summary, with the understanding that this is a malleable guide and not a formula. Or forecast your day's work with a sketch.

- Write for the purpose of exploration. Immerse yourself in the story. Even if you have a plan, don't assume you know the outcome.

- Begin by writing material that has the most energy for you. Don't necessarily begin at the beginning.

- Write in "islands" or "thought chunks." These might be independent scenes or paragraphs of exposition or simply fragments of text. Assume an inherent deep structure without striving to achieve it.

- If you're writing a longer work, place all your text in a single document. Label each separate chunk with an identifiable heading and create a document map, or use a word processing program that automatically outlines your headings. This way you can easily navigate and reposition large amounts of text.

- Don't angle toward completion. Avoid closure, especially in short pieces that will join together to make a longer work. Practice patience with incompletion.

- Use place holders. When you can't think of the right word or description or need to do research, make a note and keep moving. Momentum is more important than accuracy.

Revision Is a Form of Love

Writing for writing's sake is marvelous so long as we aren't in denial about our dreams. Most writers, whether we admit it or not, want our creations to be recognizably dynamic, in the private sphere as well as for a broader readership. We write because we want to communicate. When fear of playing to an audience or facing an audience upon completion keeps us from ever developing our work, everyone loses. The writer never experiences the wild ride of revision, nor receives revision's gifts. No readers benefit. Aborted projects may lead to energizing new projects, but aborted creativity serves no one.

Besides, we can reap the benefits of revision and still choose to keep our work private.

Revision's bad reputation is based on stereotypes and misunderstanding. As soon as we pen a thought, we've already revised an invisible, intangible wisp inside our head into visible, tangible print. Something changes. Like any creative act, writing creates simultaneously inside and outside the creator. Writing helps us receive what experiences have made of us and make something of these experiences, which is how the Jungian Ann Belford Ulanov describes the source of all aliveness. Revision brings us and our work to life. Isn't this why we initially fell in love with writing? Writing *moved* us, and what we wrote *moved* others. Writing revised our world.

When we segregate revision from idea generation or journal writing or drafting—when we assume revision is for the professionals, and especially when we imagine revision to be devoid of exploration and surprise—we do a disservice to the creative process. Revision—reseeing—begins when we pen our first thought and continues through the drafting and development of a work, into and beyond publication. Revision is the dynamic, relational work of creating and being created. Isn't this also the work of love?

Ideally, three parties are revised by our writing: the work itself, the writer, and the reader.

If I had to point to one piece of advice upon which my writing philosophy is built, it would be the fervent words children's author Jane Yolen uttered at Calvin College's Festival of Faith and Writing. She spoke about the importance of addressing faith questions in books for kids: What happens after we die? Is God real? The primary book buyers for children's authors are public schools and public libraries, which don't usually shelve faith stories. Yolen told us to write them anyway. A member of the audience challenged her: Shouldn't writers be accountable to the book buyers? Yolen got angry. "All writers are accountable to three things, in this order: First, we're accountable to the story. Second, we're accountable to ourselves. Only lastly are we accountable to our audience."

It's so easy to jumble these priorities! We place the audience first, compromising our needs and curiosity and joy. We confuse and conflate publishers with readers. We rarely consider ourselves worthy of creative investment, or we fear we're egotistical if we do. Worse yet, we don't appreciate the story itself as an entity worthy of devotion. The story: a memory, an imaginative ramble, a question pursued with characters and moments in time. "The universe is made of stories, not of atoms," writes Muriel Rukeyser. Stories are of us and beyond us. By writing stories we make our world. Stories are a source of life. They have their own energy, their own will. A first draft gives the writer and reader a vague glimpse of this source. Only time and attention—love, that is—lend that life force a body. In the beginning is a story—a mystery—and the writer loves it into being.

Exercises

Remembering the Beginning

In ten minutes, write your earliest fond memory of writing. Then reflect: What happened in that moment? What came alive?

Tracing Your Motivations

As quickly as you can, sketch a timeline of the ten most significant moments in your writing life—those moments that fundamentally shaped your relationship with writing, for good or ill. Then reflect: What initially drove you to write? How has your motivation changed over the years? When you write today, what motivations are at play?

Create a Revision Metaphor

Consider your current thoughts and feelings toward revision. What is revision like for you? Pulling teeth? Cleaning the refrigerator? Happily trudging through the woods? Write an extended metaphor describing your relationship to revision.

Locating Love

Popular science fiction author Ray Bradbury writes that feeding the muse is "the continual running after loves, the checking of these loves against one's present and future needs, the moving on from simple textures to more complex ones, from naïve ones to more informed ones, from nonintellectual to intellectual ones." What loves are you running after in your current writing project? Make a list. Then speculate about each item on the list. What might it take to nurture this love?

Excitement versus Enlivenment

Diane Millis in her book Conversation: The Sacred Art *makes a distinction between paths that merely excite us and those that truly enliven us. "What enlivens us tends to endure," she observes. Her discernment questions are good to ask of a writing project:*

- *Does the path you are considering taking expand you, stretch you beyond your comfort zone, and invite you to grow?*

- *Does the path you are considering increase your sense of connection with your subject matter, other people, and the world in which you live?*

- *Do the enthusiastic stirrings of your heart persist even as you experience obstacles and setbacks?*

Why Does It Seem So Hard?

Between each draft, new and experienced writers alike approach revision as though it's a dauntingly high hurdle. But the insurmountable problem isn't revision; it's a misconception about the creative process. With a shift in attitude, a few skills, and lots of perseverance, all writers can move beyond each draft into more developed work and a richer relationship with the writing process. We just need to unlearn the many habits that close our hearts to change.

Revision Is Not Editing

Not to blame our English teachers—I was one—but most of our rotten assumptions about revision originated early, with a teacher's red pen. Remember your first ventures onto the page? Chances are they were met not with questions, conversation, or imaginative prodding but with corrections. When our early readers reacted to spelling rather than content, they taught us that content is static. When they assigned a grade to our work, they taught us that others' judgments determine the value of our thoughts. The occasional request for revision usually meant a chance to fix mistakes.

This is why people think revision means correcting typos, considering word choice, or restructuring sentences. As a result revision seems dull, mechanical, and perfectionistic. All the fun—the buzz of invention—is over.

But that isn't revision; that's editing. By addressing the text's surface rather than probing the depths of content and craft, our early teachers taught us to attend to the mechanics of language at the expense of substance. That heaviness we sometimes feel toward a rough draft, as though the words are carved in stone, is the unfortunate result of these early lessons. We can't imagine why a draft should change, or how.

The Greatness Myth

Writers like to hold up the myth of Jack Kerouac's *On the Road* as a paradigm of possibility: He wrote it in three weeks! It was perfect! It's a great American novel! Kerouac thought so too when he rushed into Robert Giroux's office in 1955. When Giroux told him the manuscript needed editing, Kerouac insisted it was dictated "by the Holy Ghost" and stormed out. Then he spent six years revising, polishing, and shopping it around before *On the Road* found a home with Viking.

Why do we have collective amnesia about those six years? We want to slide down a shimmering writing rainbow to the pot of gold. We want to be told we're a genius; we want to knock an editor's socks off with a first draft. We're attached to the idea of Kerouac typing in an ecstatic rush and hitting the writer's jackpot because that means such ease, inspiration, and recognition are possible for us. Six years of revision tarnish the myth, as do the three years Kerouac spent taking notes and formulating his story before he began composing. Three weeks of fun appeal to us more than nine years of effort.

The myth of *On the Road* does a disservice to writers everywhere. Good stories rise up from inspiration *and* labor, over great lengths of time. Your draft, however brilliant, *can* mature and likely *must* mature before it engages an audience. That your writing will benefit from more work says nothing about your value as a human being or your skills as a writer.

Every writer needs a healthy, ambitious ego. You need chutzpah to generate an idea and consider it worthy, to get your butt into the chair, to plow through initial and many consequent drafts, and to seek publication. But the desire for greatness to come easily is the ego in hyperdrive. The ego is necessary to write; the ego's attachments interfere with life-giving creativity. No one can serve two masters.

"The impulse to improve is . . . a sign of humility, of bowing one's neck before the humbling undertaking of learning how to be worth one's salt as a writer," writes Richard Tillingast. In religious traditions, humility is the awareness of oneself as one really is. This direct, honest gaze does not come easily, as any writer who's experienced the highs of inspiration and the crashing lows of denigration can attest. But an ongoing practice of gazing at *what is* supports both our stories' growth and our own. "In humility is the greatest freedom," Thomas Merton writes in *New Seeds of Contemplation*. "As long as you have to defend the imaginary self that you think is important, you lose your peace of heart." The greatest potential for our creative work comes when we've humbly acknowledged our limitations, stopped feeding the ego, and applied our energy to the story. Only then is growth possible.

Exercise

Surrender and Letting Go

Explore in your writer's notebook: In what ways does writing help you practice surrender or letting go? What might your current project be asking you to surrender for the sake of the story?

A Whole New Devil

By the time a writer considers rewriting, the work of composing is familiar: a blank page, a tentative start, the splash of gladness when words arrive, the adrenaline rush of stumbling onto new awareness or memories or characters, the disappointment of seeing brilliant thoughts diminished in print, the satisfaction of penning that final period. We know this process. We're attached to it, for good reason. Drafting is gratifying, fun, and full of revelations. While we may admit the draft is rough, it also sparkles. Often we're reluctant to diminish that sparkle with the insult of revision. We hover over our first drafts, love and pride and self-consciousness tangling with our material. This is our baby!

Familiarity breeds fondness, along with peril. Sure, we say, the draft has flaws; sure, it's only one of a dozen ways to approach this subject; sure, in places the language is shoddy. But look at this lovely twist! And this streak of fine prose, and this clever remark! Or (here's a devilish defense) do you have any idea how much work I've invested? I couldn't possibly change it.

Resistance to rewriting a project is often stronger than resistance to starting it. "This explains," writes Peter Turchi, "why it can be so difficult for beginning writers to embrace thorough revision— which is to say, to fully embrace exploration. The desire to cling to that first path through the wilderness is both a celebration of initial discovery and fear of the vast unknown." A first draft is a thrilling, frightening foray into the wilderness. Once we've bushwhacked that path, we don't want to veer from it.

Attachment mires us. Most of us are committed to and therefore defensive about what we've created. Once we've taken one risk, we prefer not to take another.

But to foster lively, ongoing creativity, we must let the familiar go. Staying safe—the "better the devil you know" policy—does not serve anyone. We must learn a new way to work, with new material, in a new adventure. Revision is a whole different (and exciting) devil.

Revising Ourselves

Change, on the page as in life, does not happen when we're stubborn and clingy. Revision asks that we cast the small world we've created in words—and all it represents within our being—in entirely new light. As we learn to revise, we gain skills in listening, letting go, creating, communicating, enduring, and trusting our intuition. Our voice gets stronger. We honor the fullness of our creative impulses. We claim our stories despite their brokenness. We own our authority; we become authors. The changes we need to make in our text are miniscule compared with the changes revision demands of our hearts.

Good as this sounds, it's also scary. "When we feel resistance in any form, it's because we haven't fully committed to seeing what's true," writes Rosanne Bane, creativity coach and author. "We want to be thoughtless so life can be fraughtless. We want to avert our eyes." But self-deception hinders spiritual growth, and readers know when stories don't ring true or when a voice isn't authentic. Revision means drilling down to the hot core of our subject and bringing that burning substance to light. We have to face the truth, and this changes us.

No wonder we resist revision! Real creativity summons us to become more fully ourselves.

Uncertainty Is Our Friend

We humans dislike being undone. However much we enjoy writing, we find the disorderly process unsettling. We yearn for arrival or permission to quit. The state of incompletion is uncomfortable, as is vulnerability and unknowing. We have an unrelenting urge to wrap things up.

"During deep revision," poet Mark Doty writes, "the longer we can stay in the state of uncertainty, of unfolding possibility, the better." As in any prayer or meditation practice, we must learn to love, and stick with, the process. Once, when I was struggling with a prolonged depression in which I felt like I was groping my way down a dark tunnel, my therapist asked if I could see any light. I told her no. "Well, then," she replied cheerily, "You're halfway through!" Writers stumble through a lot of darkness before we begin to see our way out. It's unnerving. It's easy to despair.

Uncertainty, messiness, the sense of being overwhelmed—these states *define* creativity; they are signs that we're in the thick of things. We can welcome them and proceed regardless, harnessing discomfort as a motivating force.

Exercises

Resistance

What project or what aspect of your current project do you consider rewriting but also resist? In one column, jot down all your reasons for not working on it. In another, list the reasons to revise. What are you afraid of? What are you hopeful for? Spend some time journaling: Where do these messages come from? Why do they come to you? Which are worth heeding, and why? Which aren't, and why not?

Secret Writing Fantasies

What do you wish would happen when you sit down to write? Where do you dream your writing will go? What do you imagine would happen to you as a result? Play out these scenarios on the page. Then reflect on the origins of these fantasies. In what ways do they feed your ego? Are any parts of these fantasies born from your heart's longing?

Revision Is New Vision

If revision isn't what our English teachers taught, what is it exactly? Creativity is the ability to make new things or think new ideas; it is the capacity to see or make newness. Revision is the flourishing of creativity. It is the work of seeing with new eyes.

A word closely related to *revision* is *respect*, whose Latin roots mean "look back at" or "regard." Revision is the work of respecting creation.

For our purposes here, I refer to all drafts beyond the first as revision. But in reality writers revise as soon as an idea pops into our heads. A creative concept changes how we've previously understood the world. An initial draft takes that concept and gives it form—revises it—by embodying it in the printed word. When we lead curious, openhearted lives, **revision is a natural consequence of growth**. Taking revision onto the page allows us to participate intentionally, as active authors of our lives.

Revision Is Messy

New writers are often intimidated by the brilliance of their favorite authors—how vividly they imagine their characters, how accurately they remember the past, how gorgeous their prose. "When I am the reader," writes memoirist Patricia Hampl, "I too fall into the lovely illusion that the words before me which read so inevitably, must also have been written exactly as they appear, rhythm and cadence, language and syntax, the powerful waves of the sentences laying themselves on the smooth beach of the page one after another faultlessly." Why bother writing, we all wonder, if we can't write like *that*?

A published work is deceptively clean and not a reliable window onto the author's process. Every great work of literature sits atop journals, notes, drafts, and reader comments. What we see in print is the proverbial tip of the iceberg; the tremendous understory of seeing and reseeing keeps it afloat. Most published authors aren't unusually smart; they don't have superhuman memories or imaginations or descriptive powers. They simply work hard, over long periods, through tremendous chaos. "It still comes as a shock to realize that I don't write about what I know, but in order to find out what I know," Hampl continues. "Is it possible to convey the enormous degree of blankness, confusion, hunch, and uncertainty lurking in the act of writing?"

> Here I sit before a yellow legal pad, and the long page of the preceding two paragraphs is a jumble of crossed-out lines, false starts, confused order. A mess. The mess of my mind trying to find out what it wants to say. This is a writer's frantic, grabby mind, not the poised mind of a reader waiting to be edified or entertained.

Making peace with this messiness in a first draft is challenging enough. In revision, at least, we expect a tidier product.

In my experience, though, **revision is messier than drafting**. A second draft succeeds when it's worse than the first. Why? Because a second draft disrupts and even defiles the beautiful subconscious logic of the initial composition. But the resulting chaos opens possibilities. Consider the task of cleaning a storage closet. First you dismantle the current order—which, by the way, worked well for years—and create an even greater but temporary disaster, one that spills into the hallway. There's a bag for Goodwill, a bag for recycling, a bag for trash. A box for the junk you need to sort. Only once you've cleared some shelf space can you identify what you might yet need (bins? file folders? labels?) and imagine a new way to arrange the contents.

When I taught seventh grade, my students' writing notebooks quickly became a source of anxiety for their parents. The deeper the kids dove into their projects, the messier the notebooks got. They made additions in the margins, drew arrows to rearrange paragraphs, and crossed out whole pages. When parents expressed their concern at conferences, I'd praise the students' hard work. This is what revision looks like.

Revision Magnifies Inspiration

Every gorgeous sentence, every sparkling idea, is well worth loving. But stay open to the possibility that there's even more to love on the way. Lasting relationships between yourself and your story and between your reader and the story depend on this openheartedness.

Save a copy of your first draft and nothing you write will be lost. You can always retrieve that stunning sentence. The aha! moment at the end of your rough draft can become the premise of your second draft, and perhaps another aha! will strike you before you reach the revision's end. If a second awesome sentence comes your way, then your new draft contains two great sentences and two aha's. Fyodor Dostoyevsky wrote,

> Believe me, in all things labor is necessary—gigantic labor.
> . . . You evidently confuse the inspiration, that is, the first

instantaneous vision, or emotion in the artist's soul (which is always present), with the *work*. I, for example, write every scene down at once, just as it first comes to me, and rejoice in it; then I work at it for months and years. I let it inspire me, in that form, more than once (for I love it thus); here I add, there I take away; believe me that the scene always gains by it.

First drafts don't have a monopoly on the muse. Inspiration continues through and can be magnified by revision. In fact, revision can be *more* fun, creative, and insightful than drafting. For me, writing a first draft feels like scraping up clay with a baby spoon. In revision I play with the lump, molding it into a beautiful and effective form.

A spiritual director once told me that the greatest obstacle to an experience of God is a previous experience of God. The trouble with mystical experiences and inspired first drafts is our strong inclination to grow attached.

Revision Includes Generation

Rather than leading readers down the narrow path of a first draft, you can continue investigating the wilderness, growing more familiar with your material, before you invite anyone along. Early on it's important to ask, "What more do I have to say about this subject?" Our initial seeing comes from just one of many angles. What else is worth visiting in these woods? Sometimes adding new material expands the breadth of our story; more often it fills empty spaces within the bounds of the story. Regardless of how long-winded a first draft may be, we can always increase our awareness of the story's significance—its inner life. Generating more material helps.

Revision Changes the Writer's Role

If a first draft is a private romp in the woods, consequent drafts teach us about the flora and fauna, the geology, the contours of the landscape. Our intimacy with the subject deepens. Our respect grows. We find that the best route through the woods is likely not our first path. Only toward the end of a lengthy revision process, once we thoroughly know our material, ought we turn our attention to the needs of our readers. Revision transforms the writer from explorer to guide.

Revision Invites Revelation

Any discussion of revision points us to a hidden, tender intersection between craft and the human heart. The wisest words about writing I've ever encountered come from an introduction by Robert Frost to a 1938 volume of his collected works. "No tears in the writer, no tears in the reader. No surprise for the writer, no surprise for the reader."[1] A writer's willingness to be transformed by the process is the foundation of effective writing. If we are unwilling to be moved,

---

1   "Step by step the wonder of unexpected supply keeps growing," Frost continues. "There may be a better wildness of logic than of inconsequence. But the logic is backward, in retrospect, after the act. It must be more felt than seen ahead like prophecy. It must be a revelation, or a series of revelations, as much for the poet as for the reader."

there's no way our readers will be moved. Our searching and discoveries embed themselves in the text; they are the necessary ingredient for revelation. Neither genius nor skill can substitute.

This is why we must not just write what we know, as the old writing maxim advises, but also write toward the unknown. The unknown is too vast to conquer in one draft. To write in a way that moves others, writers must repeatedly delve into mystery, risking tears and surprise throughout multiple revisions. There's a direct link between the sustained openness of a writer's heart and the creation of enduring literature.

Openness to transformation is also essential to nurturing our love affair with writing. Despite our resistance, despite (or because of) all our labor, personal transformation brings us great and lasting pleasure, as does the evolution of our projects. We come most alive when we participate in the transformation of ourselves and our world.

Exercises

Change and the Map of Personal Experience

When have you made a behavior change that significantly altered your sense of self? Perhaps you sobered up or told the truth about your sexual identity or learned to manage your anger. Briefly summarize that story. Then explore these questions: What did this change demand of you? What was lost and what was gained? What habits or practices support this change today? How might you draw from the wisdom of this transformation as you seek to transform your writing?

You Already Know How to Revise

Consider your lifetime relationship with writing. According to this new understanding of revision, when have you revised or been revised? Write that story.

Tips for Managing Drafts

- If you're working on the computer, *do not* rewrite over a previous file. Save each draft. Take a screen shot or copy and paste your text into a new file before rewriting. This allows you to recover your initial work. (For me, this is a psychological rather than a practical trick. I rarely retrieve prose from my first draft. But knowing I can frees me to experiment.)

- Use a single computer file for each project, no matter how large. Use headings and a table of contents to organize material.

- Label draft files on the computer with the date first, beginning with the year, followed by the month—for example, 16.08Living Revision. Your drafts will then appear in chronological order.

- Periodically print and work with hard copies. We experience text differently in print than on a screen. Likewise, if you write primarily by hand, type it up to get a different perspective.

- Create a file box or drawer for your current project. Save one copy of each draft until the project is complete. Date your drafts.

CHAPTER TWO

The Long Lovely Journey

During my first years of serious writing, I labored under the conceit that *I was writing a book*. The thought was bracing; it motivated me to climb out of bed at 5:30 a.m. for half an hour of solitude before facing a classroom of seventh graders. Not until I entered my third and fourth years on the project, having given up public school teaching, did I find that my memoir was not a travel adventure about biking through Wales but rather a disconcerting reconciliation between my bisexuality and Christian upbringing; only after I revised the book multiple times did I begin to understand what was really happening: *The book was writing me*. The primary creation wasn't a memoir but the self—a self humbled by my truth and yet less afraid to claim it, a self no longer blindly controlled by my past but rather an agent in comprehending and framing it, a self in conversation with community and culture and history. My commitment to the memoir pulled me out of the closet and into public discourse.

I'm hardly alone in this experience. "Painting myself for others," Michel de Montaigne writes about his personal essays, "I have painted my inward self with colors clearer than my original ones. I have no more made my book than my book has made me." When writers write to find out what we think, we're changed. Robert Anderson describes it this way in his memoir, *Out of Denial*:

> A hand holding a pencil is drawing on a piece of paper another hand holding a pencil. The two pencil points converge, forming an endless loop in one of those curious Escher puzzles: where does the action begin and end, what is reality and what is dream or intention, who is the drawer and who is the drawn? . . . I am writing, and I am written; I tell my story, and my story tells me. It's an endless loop, this act of living and re-membering.

Within self-discovery is self-creation, the authoring of one's being. This feedback loop is especially obvious in creative nonfiction, where the subject matter is personal experience. But all genres have the potential for this intimate connection between text and self. **The best writing emerges when the stakes are high—when the author writes what's most pressing and heartfelt—because the potential for discovery is then correspondingly high**.

Oddly enough, our striving to make art often threatens its potential to become art, whereas if we strive to live more fully or become better people or participate in a bigger conversation or add meaning or beauty to the world, and if art-making is our modus operandi, we can stay healthy and actually make art. Art is a means, not an end. Or as the painter Robert Henri put it, "Art . . . is the trace of those who have led their lives." To take this a step further, creative engagement (of which art-making is one manifestation) *is* life, *is* fullness. So the deepening of our artistic practice is a path to coming fully alive—with the side benefit of inviting readers along on the journey.

I picture the creative process traveling the figure-eight curves of an infinity sign. We begin in the world, where a travel adventure or newspaper headline or grave illness or moral conundrum sets the mind's gears grinding. Quickly the work moves inward to the incubating privacy of a journal or notebook. We remember; we research; we imagine. We gather thoughts. Eventually words amass on the page. Sometimes they seem golden, sometimes lackluster. Always they're fragile, raw, and embarrassingly self-centered— rightly so, since mucking around is necessary before anything truthful or timeless can appear. Our private writing is therapeutic and transformative.

Slowly, gradually, we massage the words, granting them sequence and shape. We develop characters and ideas until they acquire some spark. We dig under and around and within our scenes, struggling to present them in the clearest, most honest light. But words are not simply a means of self-expression; they *communicate*, they bridge one soul to another, one culture to another, one era to another. Eventually we emerge from our protected space to consider an audience. **If we want the heart of our story to connect to the heart of a reader, or if we want our story to have artistic merit, we open the transformative process to others through our literary choices**. A first draft is always skin-deep, whereas revision digs in. Hearts reside in the hidden fathoms of the body. True beauty is both within and without, in striking balance.

Finally our work travels that figure-eight path out into the light. Revision transforms an interior monologue into a spirited dialogue. Our language grows considered and considerate. Rather than imagining some monolithic audience as I write, I try to picture myself and my work moving toward full participation in community.

Community holds us accountable. The possibility of a reading community invites us into artistic practice, because what makes writing artful is a hospitable, compassionate, challenging connection with others. This isn't about pandering to a market; it's about forming genuine relationships. This is why Nathaniel Hawthorne called writing an "intercourse with the world." Conversing through print requires skill and hard work—well-constructed scenes and characters, developed themes, clear organization, intentional pacing, a strong voice, correct grammar, clean mechanics. **With maturation, the work can interact independently with others; it can land back at community, where all spiritual journeys arrive**.

A book (or any shared work) has a public life separate from its author. It traverses that loop of the figure eight further out than most retiring writers like. The ensuing discomfort and elation in the author are also opportunities for the author's tears and surprise. The entire writing process, including time between projects, has the potential to transform the writer.

While our writing travels into the unfathomable realms of interiority and the far reaches of exteriority, we authors need to keep both feet in the raw, pulsing center of the infinity curve—at the grounded, openhearted crossroads. The firmer our rootedness there, the farther our reach.

For over twenty-five years I've worked with hundreds of writers as they've drafted and crafted their stories. I've also worked as a spiritual director, listening deeply to clients as they seek meaning and purpose. The questions that open a writer's heart to transformation and therefore fine writing are the same questions that open a seeker's heart: What details do you remember about that moment? What were you thinking and feeling? How do you now understand what was happening? How did this event shape you? What might it reveal about human nature? About life's great mysteries? When a writer or spiritual seeker focuses on the details, it's helpful to probe why these details matter. When a writer or seeker uses grand abstractions, the best way to unearth the truth is to ask for concrete examples.

Whether my client is an atheist striving to write well or a seeker writing to grow in spirit, the same questions help them achieve their goals. How remarkable! The creative process contains within it all the listening, solitude, rigor, and revelation of a spiritual practice. If our goal is to move our readers, poet Robert Frost suggests we open ourselves to tears and surprise. If our goal is to come more alive, deepening our humanity and sharpening our understanding of our world, writing well enough to move an audience can take us there. Either way, revision is the path.

A Timeline of the Writing Process

This timeline shows the stages of the writing process in proportion.

Of course there are writers for whom this timeline is not representative—writers who edit as they draft, writers who choose not to publish. However, for amateur writers interested in learning to write well, for most literary writers, and for all those who write as a spiritual practice, this timeline represents a realistic, life-giving sequence for a creative project's development.

First we get an inkling. We jot down notes, scenes, thoughts, and scattered bits of prose—prewriting, some call it. Ideas gestate and percolate.

Then we segue into a draft.

However long our first draft takes, we spend approximately five to ten times longer revising. The draft expands and shrinks. The content deepens. The prose tightens.

As we prepare to ship the manuscript out, we clean up the cosmetics—we edit. If we find an agent or publisher, they will oversee final development work and copyediting. At last, our words meet their audience.

This timeline also suggests a progression of priorities—a triage—that helps us be as efficient as possible. (Ha! Efficiency in the art world is relative.) The task of a first draft is to play, explore, discover. The task of later drafts is to uncover the work's heartbeat—its central, unifying theme—and support that heartbeat in every dimension of the work. The task of editing is to serve that heartbeat with elegance and efficiency.

If we skip the gestating stage, we can get bogged down while generating. If we try to perfect that first chapter before drafting the whole, we limit the draft's potential. If we edit too soon, we grow attached to beautiful language that perhaps doesn't serve the story. If we revise forever, our work never moves out into the world.

Create healthy internal organs first; figure out what pumps life into this being, help the circulatory system communicate with the nervous system in coordination with the digestive system, grow those bones good and strong, and wrap it all in skin. Finally do the hair, apply the makeup, and usher that kid out the door.

Here's another way to understand this time frame. Most of us assume that we care for the people in our lives because we love them. Studies show that the opposite is true: We come to love people more deeply as we care for them. Adoptive parents know this, as do those tending the terminally ill. Acts of nurturing elicit love. **Great love in and for a creative work is the result of great care, which can happen only with time. Our readers' love of our work penetrates only as deep as our own**.

A Humble Example: "Bloodroot"

Here is a condensed example of the evolution of an essay. I share it not because it's my best writing but because it's short, which makes the revision process more transparent. First, my rough draft:

Bloodroot, draft 1

The month before I decided to buy this stucco bungalow, I lived in the north woods and grieved daily what I would soon be leaving: sharp constellations at night, goldfinches at my window, the two-toned arch of freight train whistles, and, first thing in the spring, bloodroot blooming against the forest loam. I couldn't imagine home without that delicate, white surprise. So when I walked from my prospective house eastward toward the Mississippi, trying on the neighborhood, and cut down to a paved path skirting the gorge, with Minneapolis ten miles up river and St. Paul fifteen miles down; when I came under branches still stark but budded and found, scattered along the precarious slope, bloodroot, their leaves wide green gloves catching sunlight, each petal fleeting and perfect, the flowers became a sign: manna pointing toward home. My fragile heart would bloom here, too. With the passing of each spring, I've come to believe that curling leaves, kicked stones or drops of river water don't need divine prodding to be messengers of hope. God is as diffuse as the rest of us. White breath scattered in the humus is just one beauty I've sunk my love into. Home becomes our passion seeding the earth, sending down its roots.

I felt proud after writing this paragraph—most of my rough drafts are far worse. The more experienced you become, the better your initial drafts. Revision teaches us to find the good stuff sooner. Then I wrote in my journal:

Okay, what am I trying to say here? At first I thought of the bloodroot as a sign from the universe that I was meant to move here, or at least that this would be an okay place for me to be. Over time, though, I've come to no longer believe the world works that way. I passionately love bloodroot, and the fact that it grows in Minneapolis is a great comfort. But then I passionately love a lot of things, like flocks of crows. So it might have been the crows that spoke to me that day, or the glint of the river. Regardless, it's my love that makes the bloodroot into a sign, and not some external, divine force.

Reading this today, I'm struck by the contrast between my journal's carefree voice and the self-conscious contortions of the draft.

The journal returned me to myself. It also helped me figure out why I needed to write about bloodroot. I listened to my subject, temporarily closing the door on my perceived audience.

Here's my rewrite—not significantly different until the end. The handwritten marks are my writing group's comments.

simplify time frame

Bloodroot, second draft

writing group feedback:

The month before I decided to buy this stucco bungalow, I lived in the north woods and grieved daily what I would soon be leaving: sharp constellations at night, goldfinches at my window, the two-toned arch of freight train whistles, and, first thing in the spring, bloodroot blooming against the forest loam. I couldn't imagine home without that delicate, white surprise. So when I walked from my prospective house eastward toward the Mississippi, trying on the neighborhood, and cut down to a paved path skirting the gorge with Minneapolis ten miles up river and St. Paul fifteen miles down; when I came under branches still stark but budded and found, scattered along the precarious slope, bloodroot, their leaves wide green gloves catching sunlight, each petal fleeting and perfect, the flowers became a sign: manna leading me toward home. Since then I've come to believe that curling leaves, kicked stones or drops of river water don't need divine prodding to be messengers of hope. God is diffuse and commensurate. Had the bloodroot not been blooming that day, a flock of raucous crows might have spoken to me instead. White breath scattered in the humus is just one beauty I've sunk my love into, and love is what lends it import. Our passion seeds the earth, sending down blood-red roots.

mixed metaphor

ending too tidy, abrupt

highlight bloodroot's discovery: land here.

Note how my readers kept me accountable. My long sentence is an attempt to show off, not communicate. I need to slow down, to render the process of discovery and reveal its emotional impact. I've confused the Israelites' journey through the desert with Hansel and Gretel. I use grand abstractions to create a seemingly profound but inaccurate ending.

This last version shows two additional edits—one from me (typed), the second from my editor (handwritten).

final draft

~~The months~~ before I bought this stucco bungalow I lived in the north woods of Minnesota and grieved daily what I would soon be leaving—sharp constellations at night, goldfinches at my window, the two-toned arch of freight train whistles, and, first thing in the spring, bloodroot blooming against the forest loam. Surely the wild blossoms had been banished from paved Minneapolis. I couldn't imagine home without that delicate, white surprise.

~~Then,~~ one afternoon, I walked ~~out~~ down what would become my front ~~door~~ steps and headed east toward the Mississippi, trying on the neighborhood, looking for confirmation that I belonged; I cut down to a paved path skirting the gorge, with the down-towns of Minneapolis and St. Paul ten miles up and down river, and found there, scattered amid rusting cans and last autumn's decay, bloodroot! Each white petal was fleeting and perfect. Their wWide green gloves caught the sunlight. ~~The flowers where I least expected them were miraculous: a trail of moonlight pointing me toward home.~~ The flowers where I least expected them were a sign from heaven: a trail of white light leading me home.

In the years since then I've come to believe that curling leaves, kicked stones or drops of river water don't need divine prodding to become messengers. Had the bloodroot not been blooming that day, a flock of raucous crows might have spoken to me instead. My desire for home would have planted its own clues, regardless, between cracks in the sidewalk or among the sprawling roots of oak. White breath scattered in the humus is just one beauty I've sunk my love into; love and this longing for love compose my path. God is diffuse and commensurate, like the black midwestern soil. Desire—our own—seeds the earth, sending down its blood-red roots.

(Handwritten edits = final)

An important change in the first paragraph is the addition of my expectation that wildflowers don't grow in the city. In previous drafts, I assumed my readers shared this expectation. Since my surprise depends on this expectation, it's too important to leave unstated.

In the second paragraph I fudge geography slightly for the sake of simplicity. I've divided up my long sentence so it lands on the surprise. The metaphor still doesn't work for me, but it's adequate.

This last draft does a much better job of making my point: My "signs from God" originate in relationship; they're not an external message so much as a consequence of love. In consideration of my audience, I try to ground my theologically complex idea in the soil metaphor. Three paragraphs break up the tangled time frames. The piece functions.

From first to final draft, six months passed, even though these rewrites are far less invasive than most. I hope they illustrate how journaling, time, and others' comments can enrich a piece.

Toolbox: The Project Journal

A student recently gave me a traditional composition book made from recycled paper, labeled "The Decomposition Book." I love it. All writers need a place to break down our ideas and stir up something fertile.

A project journal is the handiest revision tool I know. The very presence of those pages in my drawer, still and pulsing with potential, influences my writing. Why? Because that notebook, which I save for the purpose of seeing my subject anew, holds the same creative promise as an initial draft. I have one hundred pages in which to tinker. That space is separate from the draft, which in my case resides in a computer file. I can be brutally honest in the journal; I can be sloppy. The project journal is my happy companion.

What goes in it? First, taking a lesson from Virginia Woolf's diaries, I use it to vent about the writing process. If I'm stuck, I write about being stuck. If I'm despairing, I make note. Over time, I recognize patterns in the emotional highs and lows of writing and find comfort in their cycles. For example, I often feel stymied between drafts, as though I'll never see my way clear to a new vision. Evidence in journal after journal that the stymied period always passes has over time eased my sense of panic. A safe place to record my process acts as a release valve and makes me more self-aware.

Second, a project journal allows me to use a natural voice without concern for the reader. My clearest, freshest self surfaces there. When I transition from draft to journal, I ground myself back in that voice. Sometimes phrases, sentences, or whole paragraphs are good enough to transfer back into my draft. More often I simply shed my pretenses, remember myself, and return to the project with greater integrity.

Third, old-fashioned pen and paper allow writers to play with manuscripts in ways a computer can't. I use my notebook to draw mind maps, bubbles of ideas that link and digress and sprawl. I make timelines to help me sort out chronology. I sketch visual representations of my work's structure so I can see its shape in its entirety. I color-code elements of the story—characters, themes, places—to find gaps and to create balance. The revision journal provides a loose visual means to experiment.

The more tools we use, the more ways we can approach our material. When I compose on the computer, my prose is fast, sloppy, and bold. When I write by hand, I pay more attention to words; I pause more often; I'm more apt to be honest. More areas of the brain are involved in writing by hand than by keyboarding. When we use multiple modalities, we increase our chances of apprehending material of substance.

Lest you consider me a Luddite, you should know that for every project I also keep a computer file that acts as a journal. There I harbor the darlings I'm unwilling to kill—that is, when I cut passages from my draft, they move to the purgatory of my revision journal, where they usually languish. But their continued existence puts me at ease. I always review them to decide whether my judgment was sound before moving to the next draft.

When I'm interrupted by an inspiration in the middle of composing, the computer file helps me move quickly from draft to journal. I keep to-do lists here. At the end of a writing period, I jot down incomplete thoughts, lingering ideas, details I want to plant, and a possible agenda for the next day. The electronic version of my revision journal is a catchall, a junk drawer for stuff that might be useful, and a place to track the tasks ahead.

Regardless of where or how we keep a revision journal, the aim is to create a retreat for ourselves—a haven where we can see our work with fresh perspective and from which we can return to composing with renewed vigor. Here we ask the hard questions: What am I afraid of? What am I really trying to say? What's standing in my way? Here we get the benefits of writing quickly and unself-consciously. "In your diary, if you write fast, as though you vomited your thoughts on paper, you will touch only those things that interest you," Brenda Ueland says. "You will skip from peak to peak. You will sail over the quagmire of wordy explanations and timidly qualifying phrases." You get to the point. Carol Bly also advocates journal writing:

> In recent years I have been telling student writers that in addition to keeping journals and taking notes for the works they hope to write, they should keep journals and take notes as a way of developing their own philosophy. . . . Each mind wants to have a somewhat unified theory, whatever it can manage. The mind should be willing to change its worldview as fast as a bat can dip or suddenly soar, but at any one time, the mind should have its own way of looking at the world.

> Keeping a journal that no audience reads allows us to grapple with our subject matter or with the rough spots of daily life until we've formed a philosophy. The mind *wants* unity; it needs space and permission to find it.

> The journal acts as a handbag. In it we tote reckless honesty. We can pull out that open, freewheeling mindset whenever there's a need. The journal reconnects us with the wellspring of our creativity.

Time, the Natural Reviser

Most writers rankle at interruptions. We want to keep our projects moving; we're eager to be done.

I beg you: Be patient. Franz Kafka is said to have posted a sign above his writing desk that read, simply, WAIT. The best revisions I've seen have resulted not from determined grunt work but from stepping away. To see a manuscript with fresh eyes, get some distance.

Why? The questions we ask, the themes or images we investigate, the pressing urge to write—these are not the whims of a particular project; they are born of our personality, history, and current struggles. Writing is a waking dream; it is peopled with parts of ourselves, set in places that haunt us, and compelled by our deepest misgivings. If there is continuity between our lives and writing, time away from a project becomes research. A draft is a posited theory; we can step back, test that theory, and develop it without ever putting pen to page. By turning away from a draft, Janet Burroway suggests, we mail it to our unconscious—a source we certainly need to consult.

Lenore Franzen, a student of mine, calls the space between drafts "recess." Every elementary school teacher knows that time spent running around the playground amps up students' learning. Give yourself a writing recess.

Active and Passive Disengagement

Lest you think this elaborate avoidance, let me distinguish between active and passive disengagement from writing. In active disengagement, we stay connected to our work. Sometimes we choose to set it aside; sometimes we must. Life may intervene with illness, birth, death, or other disruptions. But in active disengagement, writing remains our primary creative endeavor. A project demands attention not because we *should* be writing but because we *love* writing. We are curious about the outcome. We can't help but think about our project.

Poet Elizabeth Bishop is an excellent model of active disengagement. She pinned her incomplete drafts to a bulletin board, waiting for months and sometimes years to fill in missing words. Susan Snively writes that Bishop's "refusal to hurry a poem was, among other things, a way to say that the poem's special life had to be honored above her own need for closure or publication." Bishop heeded the poem's timeline, not her own.

According to Robert Boice's research, "The most creative, imaginative individuals display unique talents for avoiding premature closure; they put off final decisions about organizing ideas while maintaining high standards for (1) the quality of the materials they collect and for (2) the purpose of collecting them. In other words, they wait." Active disengagement is like the pause you take after stirring yeast into warm water or during the bread dough's rising. Waiting is an essential step.

In passive disengagement, writers' fundamental loyalty shifts away from a particular project or from writing itself. Passive disengagement is a sign that we should move on. I find no fault in this.

Many other endeavors are equally worthy—raising children, protecting our environment, working for social justice, healing the sick. But for those driven to write, regardless of talent or success, writing ranks among our most important activities. Usually our mistrust of this fact plays itself out in mundane distractions—e-mail, dishes, laundry. If you're drawn to write and aren't writing because of guilt or small distractions, examine your priorities. The desire to write has profound origins. We ought always to heed the creative source.

One way to stay actively disengaged is to test your project against your lived life—in your relationships, out in the natural world, in the context of history or science or psychology, or within whatever event has pulled you away from your writing. What questions or images from your project continue to be relevant? A worthy investment extends beyond the page. I've found that interruptions usually provide information and challenges appropriate to my writing—for example, in a break between revisions of my midwifery novel, I witnessed my adopted daughter being born and experienced firsthand what it's like to become a mother. In earlier drafts I was able to imagine these events fairly well, but experience gave my writing texture it would not have had otherwise.

After too much time, active disengagement can slide into passive disengagement. During times of active disengagment, be sure to feed the creative work of the unconscious with reading, art, conversation, or any activity that nourishes your subject or craft.

Conceptual Leaps between Drafts

When I taught seventh grade, I faced the challenge of working with concrete thinkers developmentally incapable of revising creative work. My students wrote stories with summarized conversation; I then taught a lesson on dialogue, walked the class through exercises, and asked them to revise a scene. With few exceptions, the twelve-year-olds couldn't successfully integrate dialogue. But when they started fresh with a new story, their characters started talking.

"Art lies embedded in the conceptual leap between pieces, not in the pieces themselves," write David Bayles and Ted Orland. Certainly that's where artistic development lies. I would argue that these conceptual leaps occur whenever we remove ourselves from our work and then reenter from a fresh angle. Or as Brenda Ueland states, "Don't be afraid of writing bad stories. To discover what is wrong with a story write two new ones and then go back to it." Here's my take on Bayles and Orland's wisdom: Art lies in the conceptual leaps between drafts, and leaps like this need time.

Surrendering to Time

Perhaps the kindest—and most helpful—review I ever received came from Mary Rose O'Reilly, author of *The Barn at the End of the World*: "I can imagine that [Elizabeth] has spent many hours staring out the window until she arrives at a lived-synthesis of what the great religions and irreligions have to tell us about the nature of the sacred." I don't know about the synthesis, but I can attest to staring out the window. And hours writing and then deleting what I'd written. And hours journaling for no eyes other than my own. And years revising.

"Art is long," writes Henry James. "If we work for ourselves of course we must hurry. If we work for *her* we must often pause." Immersed in our culture of instant gratification, I'm as easily seduced as the next blogger by the possibility that my words might rattle around in a reader's brain within an hour of their composing. But I also know the profound, evolutionary movement of a longer project, where readership is hypothetical, a decade isn't an unreasonable time frame, and the exploratory possibilities are endless. Henry James makes this sound noble—we're serving Art!—but for most of us, uncertainty about the artistic nature of our work packs those years and all those pauses with angst. Better to be done with it, receive a flash of social media feedback, and feel our efforts validated.

Significant creation asks us to surrender to time—to release our needs for completion and affirmation and inhabit a process that rarely unfolds the way we'd like. As uncomfortable as this makes me, I'm also certain that little else is as worthwhile. Given the escalating speed of our culture, any work that forces us to pause, gaze out the window, and trust the secret recesses of our subconscious to arrive at lived syntheses is increasingly valuable. Art is long, as is growing asparagus, learning to bake a soufflé, establishing a meditation practice, raising a child, participating in democracy, and most activities that comprise a well-lived life. When writers despair of ever finishing their books, I sympathize—it's hard not to be done!—and **I rejoice in projects so worthy and rich that they demand whole chapters of our lives**.

Rest Restores Us

Observing the sabbath is a time-tested spiritual practice: Rest replenishes energy, restores perspective, allows us to hear the "still small voice," and grants us freedom and flexibility. Rest revises us. In the writer's life, pauses in a project's progress are small sabbaths. We stare out the window; we walk around the block; we set our writing aside for the weekend. Small breaks like these, as well as longer pauses throughout the development of a project, are essential to a sustainable artistic practice. Rest revitalizes our work.

Exercises

Rest and the Map of Personal Experience

In what areas of your life are you good at resting? Choose one and explore it. Does rest come naturally here or did you have to learn to allow it? What happens to your body, mind, and spirit when you step away from work? How might you apply this wisdom to your writing?

Rest and Writing

If you have some experience writing, remember a time when you were forced to set a project aside temporarily. In what ways was this interruption a detriment or benefit to that project? To your overall work as a writer?

Is It Good Enough?

Over the years, hundreds of writers have handed me work and asked, "Is this good enough?" The question can take different forms—Do I have talent? Is it publishable? Should I keep going?—and always leaves me tongue-tied. Good enough for what? Why am I—why is anyone—assumed to have authority to pronounce writing worthwhile?

When I was in college, a professor (and award-winning novelist) declared that my writing wasn't good enough to pursue professionally. It was a blow, but not as bad as you might imagine. What he didn't know—and what I clearly *did* know—was that I had no choice. I had to write. My need was born of personality, curiosity, gratitude for writing's healing powers, an obsession with stories, and dependence on writing as my best form of prayer. I never stopped writing nor stopped valuing the act of writing because I simply *couldn't*.

Over the twenty-five years that followed, I, like every writer who has shipped her work out to be judged, have received a phenomenal amount of rejection. Publishers and grantors and contests have rejected me so much I've come to expect it. Meanwhile, I watch contradictions abound in the writing world: Poorly written books hit the best seller list; agents drop celebrated literary authors; readers tell me about unrecognized books that have changed their lives; writers with extraordinary talent choose not to share their projects with anyone; self-published books gain respect; and thousands of closeted writers put pen to page daily, faithfully, regardless of outcome. The world does not operate as though *good* equals success, worthiness, moral strength, and art. Nor does *bad* equal failure, worthlessness, moral weakness, and trash.

All this has taught me where *not* to look for confirmation of writing's worth: Egotistical professors. The publishing world. Any reader you don't know or respect. The market. Sure, external affirmations are great, but I've yet to meet anyone for whom they satisfy that perennial, aching self-doubt.

"Is it good enough?" is an exceedingly misguided question. It assumes writing is static when, in fact, most creative projects can be improved. It is predicated on a dualism that deems some projects and writers more worthy than others. Of course lots of art *is* high quality, but quality is only one part of art's value. Other, perhaps more important, factors are the personal benefits of the writing process, the risks and surprises of a new experiment, the naming of a truth, the capacity to move readers, and any positive social impact that results. We often forget that our failures can bear unexpected fruit.

I refuse to answer questions about good and bad because I abide by the poet Richard Broderick's wisdom that judgment is the death of the imagination, and that imagination is our most critical tool for remaining human. Besides, quality writing comes more from hard work than from talent. Instead I ask writers, "Is it worth it to you?" If a project merits your whole heart, it's worthwhile. The good opinions of respected readers are all gravy. An important part of becoming a writer is learning to sidestep the world's judgment and give yourself completely to what *you* cherish.

Another way to approach the insecurity lurking behind the question "Is it good enough?" is to embrace the flawed nature of our work. I appreciate the novelist Ann Patchett's description of this practice. A book composed in her head but not yet written, she says, is like an oversized butterfly of indescribable beauty, "so wild and loyal in its nature that my love for this book, and my faith in it as I track its lazy flight, is the single perfect joy in my life."

But then Patchett begins writing.

When putting it off has actually become more painful than doing it, I reach up and pluck the butterfly from the air. I take it from the region of my head and I press it down against my desk, and there, with my own hand, I kill it. It's not that I want to kill it, but it's the only way I can get something that is so three-dimensional onto the flat page. Just to make sure the job is done I stick it into place with a pin.

Imagine running over a butterfly with an SUV. Everything that was beautiful about this living thing—all the color, the light and movement—is gone. What I'm left with is the dry husk of my friend, the broken body chipped, dismantled, and poorly reassembled. Dead. That's my book.

The ability to withstand the disappointment, humility, and grief at the inevitable brokenness of our writing is what distinguishes "real writers" (a term I use carefully) from those who simply want to write. "Only a few of us are going to be willing to break our own hearts by trading in the living beauty of imagination for the stark disappointment of words," Patchett writes. The endeavor is doomed. Life on the page will always pale in comparison to the vibrant life of the imagination.

The key to enduring, as an artist and human, is learning how to weather the death of that butterfly and forgive ourselves for killing it. Patchett continues: "I can't write the book I want to write, but I can and will write the book I am capable of writing. Again and again throughout the course of my life I will forgive myself." We are always less intelligent or creative or precise or kind than we want to be, and doubly so on the page. This grief of constantly facing down our inadequacies, Patchett believes, is what keeps people from writing. I'm grateful for her insight, that forgiving ourselves and proceeding with the task at hand is a fundamental part of living and writing well.

I have a hunch that beneath the question "Is it good enough?" lurks the foundational, existential question, "Do I matter?" Spiritual practices of every tradition teach us to turn our attention away from outcomes toward the practice itself—to the kneeling, the breathing, the prayers, the release of thought. Writing is no different. Again and again, writing asks that we see ourselves as we are and our work as it is, then turn our attention back to the process. Ultimate value can be found only in the present.

Exercise

Forgiveness and the Map of Personal Experience
Write about a time when you messed up (in a relationship, a job, school-work, or a project) and then eventually forgave yourself. What made forgiveness possible? How did this affect your future endeavors? How might the lessons from this experience apply to your writing today?

Enduring Discomfort

After allowing my novel to rest for half a year, I launched back in to restructure the first hundred pages, reshape the personality of the main character, and change her reasons for making a pivotal decision. As I revised, I experienced the complicated joy of being immersed in a project. I find the sensation to be one of absolute concentration coexisting with absolute rebellion. I move into the cosmos of the book and see nothing beyond its boundaries. And I squirm. I need a glass of water, and then ice, then a coaster. I clip my toenails. When these powerful, contrary forces rise up, I know I'm in the heat of writing.

This discomfort reminds me of meditation, how part of me is drawn into the vast oblivion of silence and another part fights mightily to maintain the perceived safety of selfhood. The same con-templative muscles are at work. **When we write, the true self longs to surrender into a story, where it thrives and knows itself inte-**

gral to the larger human story. Meanwhile the false but righteous self fights to maintain its identity. In such moments, we reside at the fulcrum between our temporal, physical plane and eternity. It's thrilling and unpleasant, ecstatic and unbearable.

"I think that writers must try not to avoid knowing what is happening," Anne Sexton says. "Everyone has somewhere the ability to mask the events of pain and sorrow. . . . But the creative person must not use this mechanism any more than they have to in order to keep breathing." Why? Our stories can be true only when we look directly, simply, and clearly at reality. "We must somehow take a wider view, look at the whole landscape, really see it, and describe what's going on here," Annie Dillard writes in *Pilgrim at Tinker Creek*. "Then we can at least wail the right question into the swaddling band of darkness, or, if it comes to that, choir the proper praise." Revising is the contemplative practice of seeing and reseeing "what's going on here," then representing it on the page.

A writer's capacity to tolerate discomfort, including violent bursts of elation and anguish, determines how deeply and for how long it is possible to reside in the generative state. Discomfort is the forerunner of growth. Consider the endurance Junot Diaz needed to write *The Brief Wondrous Life of Oscar Wao*.

> The novel had me lost the entire process. The beginning only revealed itself at the end. Very frustrating to find yourself having to start at the beginning again, but that's how this writing game is. Rarely anything linear about it. In the end I handed the book to my editor convinced that what I had written was a colossal failure. I spent the next eight months demoralized about the eleven years I had wasted

on the book. Even after the awards, etc., it took a long time before I let myself look on the novel with any kindness.

Such an emotional rollercoaster ride tells us nothing about the worth of our process or product. "Write a little every day," advises Isak Dinesen, "without hope and without despair." Hope is hope for the wrong thing, as T. S. Eliot so wisely reminds us, as is despair. We must walk the middle path.

Fortunately, this is a skill we can develop. I can acknowledge my body's restlessness without leaving my writing chair; I can recognize my ego's rebellion and still immerse myself in the project. I can tolerate my dissatisfaction with the quality of my work and continue writing. While writing, we choose again and again to be uncomfortable, going against instinct and social norms and, possibly, good sense. **Discomfort gives rise to our best work**. If we can hold paradox in our bodies, we can illuminate paradox inside our stories. If we can practice walking the middle way on the page, we're more likely to walk it in our lives.

Exercises

Blessed Unrest
Strengthening our capacity to tolerate discomfort is an important part of becoming an author. "No artist is pleased," Martha Graham says. "There is only a queer divine dissatisfaction, a blessed unrest that keeps us marching and makes us more alive than any other human beings." Make a list or mind map of the many ways the current state of your project makes you uncomfortable. Then reflect: How is this discomfort a blessing?

Good Angel, Bad Angel

Consider the aspect of writing that is most uncomfortable for you. Write an imaginary dialogue between your good angel (the part of you that longs to immerse yourself in your project) and your bad angel (the part of you that resists mightily). What do they have to say—to you and to each other? What happens when they transcend their categories of "good" or "bad"?

CHAPTER THREE

So What?

Insidious, persistent, biting, the simple question "So what?" infects almost everyone who writes for an audience. It stops our pen midstroke. It gnaws at our confidence. It keeps private scribblers in the safe haven of their journals, where no one can question the value of their efforts. It infests classrooms, whole cultures even, undermining the generative instinct because it requires that we justify our time. Too many of us believe creative work is not inherently worthy.

Only the most insensitive writing teacher scrawls "So what?" in the margins of a student's work. Any mentor with half a heart knows that red ink seeps through paper to mark indelibly the writer's self. But now that I have twenty-five years of teaching under my belt, I know that, if I care about the well-being of the humans under my instruction, if I care about the quality of literature entering the world, my primary job rests on the "So what?" question. Good writing requires that we ask it. Our capacity to flourish as writers depends on an answer.

The Outer Story

When I begin working with a writer I ask, "Why? Why are you writing?" This question is a kinder version of "So what?" It scratches the surface, which is where every excavation begins.

"Because I want my grandchildren to know me."

"Because I have to."

"Because it's good therapy."

"Because I want to help others going through [treatment for addiction, breast cancer, mental illness, their children's teenage years]."

"Because the world needs this story."

"Because it's fun."

All good reasons. Any piece of writing may be sparked by a dozen motivations, all worth airing. I want to hear the surface explanation, the public face of "So what?," the reason you give your in-laws or a politely interested cocktail party guest (who will then ask, predictably, "Are you published?"). This external explanation gives rise to what I call **the *outer story*, the characters and events that make up the plot**.[2] *What* do you want your grandkids to know? How you survived the Depression? Why you disowned their mother and then reconciled years later? What it's like to grow old? *What* story does the world need? The one you've imagined about the year 2020, when cellphones are cyberimplants and oceans have risen to alarming levels? The one you've lived, about being a person of color in twenty-first century America? *Why* is writing this fun? Because

---

2   Characters are the people who inhabit your story whether or not the story is fiction. Plot is the progression of interlocking events that move a story forward. More on these in Chapter 9.

entering a quirky scenario in the shoes of a sleuth or a stripper or a sea captain is a trip?

Our external motivations yank us out of bed early enough to fill a few pages before the morning commute. They push us through a first draft. They are real.

Nevertheless, they're rarely deep enough to sustain us through the prolonged effort of developing a project. Socially acceptable reasons for creativity are thin. They look self-consciously outward, striving to place the generative urge in a capitalistic context or justify it with the goal of personal or societal betterment. Rarely do these reasons help with or nurture our love for the writing process.

The Inner Story and the Heartbeat

When people carve out an hour of a productive day to enter the empty field of a white page, they need the guidance of longing to find the way. Beneath our external justifications for writing are secret internal motivations, and beneath these are subconscious impulses and great, pulsing mysteries we sense but cannot say. These appear in our writing's *inner story*. **The inner story is that current of emotion and thought that moves in and through the plot**. It's where passion and fear and drive lurk—motivations powerful enough for the long haul and rich enough to make the work worthwhile. The deeper we dig into why we write, the nearer we approach the dynamic source that fuels our work.

Once I interviewed a writer who was stymied by a memoir about surviving ovarian cancer. I asked her why she was writing it.

"For the money," she answered.

I broke the bad news.

She backpedaled; she knew the writer's plight. "For recognition," she said.

I gave her credit for honesty—most writers want fame but few state it so baldly. Still, I asked, was this reason enough to spend hundreds of lonely hours in front of a computer revisiting chemotherapy?

Then she told me a story. When she was going through treatment, she concluded that nobody would miss her should she die. She wasn't significant to anyone. She decided to write a book because she wanted to matter.

I paused. The air vibrated with her honesty. I felt reverent, and told her so. While she had a ways to go to put this stake front and center in her writing (that is, to harness her external story to this internal engine so it could pull the action forward), she had exposed information that was absolutely essential to writing well. She'd revealed what I call a piece's *heartbeat*, or its dominant theme. If she writes her book as an attempt to get the reader to care about her, it will flop. But if her book asks why she hasn't mattered and what it means to matter and how a life-threatening illness can elicit the significance of living, the book has a chance of working—of *mattering*.

What's at Stake?

The expression "at stake" likely hearkens back to a post on which gambling wagers were placed. The expression also evokes the practice of burning people at the stake, usually for their beliefs. Your stake is something valuable you risk losing, like your life.

Where is your heart on the line? What depends on this story's unfolding? Why does this story have a grip on you? To find a piece's inner story or heartbeat, I find it helpful to investigate the writer's stake in a project—the emotional relationship to the subject matter.

When I ask what's at stake, I want to know what the writer is seeking in the material. Underneath every lasting literary endeavor is a person's genuine encounter with an idea or an experience. Without emotional connection to our content, we might convey content to a reader but we've no reason to explore it. And impassioned exploration is what makes stories engaging to both writer and reader.

Answers to the "What's at stake?" question are instructive. They point to material that matters:

"I know human suffering has meaning, but I'm not sure what. I want to find out."

"I'm curious about how anger governs people."

"Why did I end up the person I am today?"

When we explore our stake in a subject, we identify reasons powerful enough to sustain us through the writing process. We face away from the audience and look directly at the stuff of the story.

An author's stake determines the story's emotional integrity. The more heartfelt the author's participation, the richer the emergent truth. There are direct links between why we write, how we write, and what we write.

As I move through longer projects, I repeatedly ask myself what's at stake. My answers change with each draft, growing more direct and instructive. After working on my novel for five years, after finding an agent to represent it, after receiving my first round of rejections from editors, I asked myself yet again what was at stake. The story had helped me understand the tug-of-war between fear and faith and how faith functions outside a religious tradition— questions I ask all the time from my perch at the edge of Christianity. But this time I came up with a new and surprising answer. The novel is about a midwife whose birth has a profound effect on how she delivers babies. As I wrote it, I'd repeatedly thought about my own uneventful birth. But now I thought instead about my mother, who was a preemie in the 1940s and spent six weeks in the hospital after her mother had returned home. Circumstances in my novel were different, but the stakes for my mother and my character were similar: their connection to their mothers, their sense of selfhood, the direction their lives took, all marked by what happened at their births. Now my own stake was not just theoretical but also personal: I bear the mark of abandonment in my mother's infancy. No wonder I'd spent the previous five years tracing the consequences of early trauma in my character! This insight helped me dig into the novel's emotional core and guided my revision.

"We write stories not because we have answers but because we have questions. The writing of a story *is* the wrestling with the angel," says beloved children's author Katherine Paterson. The best response to "So what?" or "What's at stake?" is another question, an unanswerable one that startles us from our sleep or makes us laugh or lasts lifetimes. It pains us; it unleashes affection. Every writing project is an attempt to give words to the unnamable bond between the author's heart and subject matter. Our struggles to articulate this are understandable. Writing itself changes the stakes.

So the most important answers to the "So what?" question are profoundly private. In one of the great paradoxes of writing well, we first must turn our backs on the audience. We must locate our single burning coal of desire.

Exercise

Asking Why

Journal: Why are you writing your current piece? How does this subject terrify you, compel you, haunt you, or jerk you into uncharted territory? In other words, what's at stake for you? Our stake in a project is our relationship to the content, not to the product. What do you hope to learn or discover or resolve?

Regulating Awareness of the Audience

Life-giving as it may seem to imagine ourselves and our writing moving toward full participation in community, in reality we're disrupted by thoughts about our readers:

"What will my mother think?"

"I'm writing a great American novel!"

"Who gives a rat's ass?"

"My boss will be awestruck by all she didn't know about me."

Audience can be a hidden part of oneself, a younger or future self, or a beloved who has died; it can be a child or loved one or others who have endured a similar struggle; it can be a niche community or the blogosphere or the vast anonymous public. Good or bad, encouraging or destructive, the audience looms over our shoulders as we write. Learning to regulate our relationship to an audience is key to a healthy writing practice.

Some writers are stimulated by an audience. A particular reader's need or a call for submissions or a topic in public discourse can spark your imagination. When an audience motivates you, by all means write to that audience. But be careful. What are you *not* writing because of this audience? *How* aren't you writing? Do you find yourself hoping the writing highlights *you*—your smarts, your significance—rather than the story? Kissing up to a potential publisher is easier than exercising your own dazzling imagination. Really, what about writing delights you? When audience supports your creative exploration, use it. When it doesn't, leave it in the dust.

For most writers, awareness of an audience too early in the writing process is crippling. We censor and perform. We cower, or show off. We skirt the truth. We deny our brilliant but quirky inner voice liberty of expression. "If the soul is thinking audience, audience, audience," Carol Bly writes, "it cannot at the same time be inquiring of itself, kindly but firmly, 'What are we doing here?'" Memoirist Cheri Register insists that

> the first draft has to be an emptying out of all truths, some so closely held that we can't see them until we get them down on paper. If we don't do this, uncontrollable revelatory outbursts or the tension of secrecy itself will impede the work. This doesn't mean we are obligated to tell all to everyone, but that we cannot select the truths worth telling or find the best form in which to convey them until we've done an honest and careful self-examination.

All writers risk exposing their psyches to the reader. We risk airing dirty laundry. We risk making gargantuan mistakes. And we need to hazard such risks to ferret out material that matters.

Best to do this work first in private.

So: We need a free, safe space. The purpose of prewriting and early drafts is to be messy, dazzling, heretical, revolutionary, stupid, outrageous, and embarrassing—in other words, creative. We need to serve the story first.

Cultivating Privacy

As writers conceive, draft, and begin reworking projects, I suggest that they surround themselves with a protective cloud of privacy— and unknowing. I imagine the cloud like this:

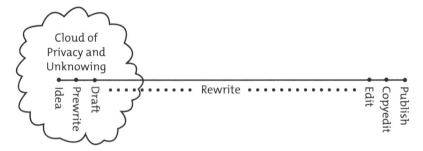

While in this space, anything goes. Write what you want, when you want, how you want, for no one other than yourself. Even Strunk and White, masters of polished prose, advise us to "never seek to know the reader's wants. Your whole duty as a writer is to please and satisfy yourself, and the true writer always plays to an audience of one." Only in the gluttonous work of drafting without consideration for others' needs can you locate your hot coal of desire.

Orhan Pamuk believes this solitary self-exploration is defining. In his speech upon accepting the 2006 Nobel Prize, Pamuk said, "A writer is someone who spends years patiently trying to discover the second being inside him, and the world that makes him who he is.

. . . To write is to turn this inward gaze into words, to study the world into which that person passes when he retires into himself, and to do so with patience, obstinacy, and joy." The path to art-making first passes through this seemingly selfish territory. **True solitude, as it turns out, draws us into communion with others just as true communion with others draws us back into solitude**.

"Follow the ache," Cheri Register teaches. Listening for the ache is simply too difficult against the ambient expectations of family members, writing teachers, possible book publishers, and a vast hypothetical public.

Beginning writers have the advantage here. For them, writing is a natural extension of the self. They don't experience separation between the ache in their guts and the black marks on the page. Because publication seems unlikely, they write for fun or catharsis or revelation. When my students say that writing is good therapy, I say, "Great!" Early in the writing process, we want the passion high, the emotions raw, the drive fierce. We want a full-throttle, high-stakes, wholehearted relationship with our work.

Writers with some publications under their belt have a much harder time returning to the cloud of privacy. They've already encountered readers, seen reviews, and watched their work circulate. Audience is no longer hypothetical. When drafting, they need robust willpower to set the future reader aside and "play to an audience of one." They must forget the reader and ask, as though for the first time, how does my life depend on this project?

A writer's best work is urgent and sincere. We don't want our writing to flirt with our life, we don't want casual dating, we want head-over-heels love leading to a lasting marriage. This is why I call that initial, private space the cloud of privacy and unknowing. The more we *don't* know at the outset, the more potential there is for surprise. By dismissing the audience early on, we cultivate a comfort —an intimacy, even—with *not knowing*. Only then is there room for the give-and-take with mystery—with the story itself.

"Write with the door closed, rewrite with the door open," Stephen King recommends. But this advice oversimplifies. I would say, rather, write with the door closed to thoughts of future readers and slowly, carefully, nudge it open.

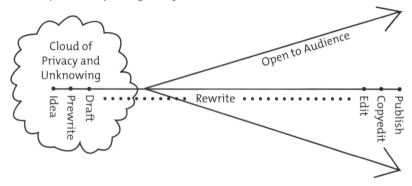

Note in the illustration how the formative stage is protected while the advanced stages invite increasing consideration of others. This gradual opening of our work is good discipline. Concern about your family's reaction to your memoir is deadly when you're drafting but important before you ship the manuscript to publishers. You can be a miserable speller or sentence constructor early on but not when sharing a manuscript with a writing group. When your inner critic tries to trip you up with self-consciousness (Who cares? Such bland prose! Such shallow thinking! What will so-and-so think?), file these concerns away. I mean this literally: Write them down in your notebook so your brain can move on. You can deal with them at the appropriate stage in the writing process.

"I am looking for stories in which the self-absorption needed by any writer in order to write has been transcended, making room for the reader to make his or her own interpretations," writes Kathleen Norris. Allow yourself time for self-absorption, then transcend it. Conversely, transcend your preoccupation with what others will think, then gradually, intentionally, consider your audience.

You can shut the door to your audience as often as you like, returning to those techniques—venting in the project journal, drafting in that cloud of privacy and unknowing—that grant you freedom. Tote that protective cloud along like a friendly balloon.

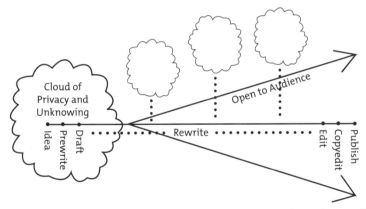

Here's the trick to sustaining a joyful, healthy relationship with writing through revision and beyond publication: *Never abandon your space of curiosity, freedom, and love*. Our work may travel outward to meet an audience. *We* may meet that audience as well, which is a tremendous privilege. But the source of a writer's well-being is that safe place where we can be intimate, honest, and adventurous. We neglect it at our peril.

Exercises

Privacy and the Map of Personal Experience

In what dimension of your life are you adept at inhabiting a cloud of privacy? In what arena are you able to try new things and make mistakes undisturbed by concern for what others will think? Consider your finances, sex life, family life, faith life, interior decorating, and so on. What makes freedom possible in this arena? How might this freedom inform your writing?

Sidelining the Audience

If concerns about real or imaginary readers come to you as you write, jot them down in your project journal. Later, freewrite in response. Who do you imagine lurking at the other end of your writing? Why? In what ways is this audience hindering or serving you? When in the writing process might be a good stage to consider this audience?

Your Inner Critic

Draw a representation of your inner critic in the center of a blank piece of paper. What are this critic's messages? Quickly, without thought or judgment, write them around the critic. Once you've exhausted the critic's resources, step back. Organize these messages into two categories: those that are hurtful and seemingly unhelpful and those that perhaps could be helpful at some stage in the writing process. Draw a timeline of the writing process and place these messages at points when they most need to be addressed. Then give yourself permission to ignore them until then.

Investigate the origins and evolutions of the hurtful and seemingly unhelpful messages in your journal. Dialoguing with such messages can diffuse their power and expose trace elements of truth worth heeding.

CHAPTER FOUR

Becoming an Author

When writers, especially beginners, first generate a draft, it feels like an extension of the self. Identity is bound up with ink. We write what matters most. There are no boundaries between writer and what's written.

Compare this to the bound text that lands in a reader's hands. The writer has fallen away. Writing is no longer a verb; it's a noun—a thing. Readers don't need the living author to mediate their encounter with a book. The nexus of creativity happens between the reader and the text.

What transforms our stories from disorganized extensions of our egos to independent entities able to move us and our readers? Revision. **The journey through drafts moves us from powerlessness to power—from being controlled by our stories to being active creators—from having an idea to being an author**. How does this happen?

When I work with therapists or Twelve Step participants or those who have repeatedly and intentionally shared their life stories with others, I'm always delighted by how writing surprises them. They remember new details. They pair memories in unexpected ways. They find themes that give them fresh focus. Writing may be therapeutic, but it is different from therapy; it uses different muscles, taps different memories, and demands of us a different wholeness.

According to James W. Pennebaker, a professor of psychology at the University of Texas, the act of writing about emotionally charged memories is directly linked to our physical health. In his studies with Sandra Beall, Pennebaker found that, among students who wrote fifteen minutes a day for four days in a row, those who were instructed to write about both a traumatic event and their emotional response felt significantly more miserable during the writing and significantly freer four months later than those who wrote about trivial subjects or who only wrote the emotions triggered by a trauma or only wrote about the events of the trauma. Those students who linked feelings to events in their writing decreased their visits to the student health center by 50 percent. Louise de Salvo, author of *Writing as a Way of Healing*, summarizes their findings in this way: "Only writing that describes traumatic events and our deepest thoughts and feelings about them, past and present, is linked with improved immune function, improved emotional and physical health, and behavioral changes indicating that we feel able to act on our own behalf." Amazingly, de Salvo continues, "the more writing succeeds as narrative— by being detailed, organized, compelling, vivid, lucid—the more health and emotional benefits are derived from writing."

I'm not aware of any similar studies that involve writing fiction, although the healing, humanizing work of *reading* fiction is well proven. If we're more empathetic and able to sustain moral complexity after having read a novel, surely we can gain such benefits by writing one.

What's going on here? When we keep our stories inside, they roil around and control our lives. Events from childhood, conscious or not, dictate our behavior. A shameful secret held close over years eats at our sense of identity, governs our choices, and causes us to generate more shameful secrets. Untold, such secrets wield terrible power. Louise de Salvo calls depression "a complex story that hasn't been told."

Once we begin talking about our inner stories, they lose a bit of their power. When a friend hears our shameful secret and laughs in sympathy, the shame dissipates. Or if the friend shares her secret in response, we feel less lonely.

Part of the reason therapy works is that the therapist serves as a stage for working with memories. The therapist hears a story, holds it, reflects on it, and helps us to see it in new ways. The professional makes room for our story to exist outside ourselves where we can work with it. Done well and over time, this can radically change our relationship to the past and our present well-being.

The page also serves as a stage, although a more permanent one than the therapist's listening ear. Written words transform a feeling or thought or memory or imaginative riff into a physical object. They mirror our stories back to us. These stories then exist outside ourselves as *things*.

At first these *things* seem inevitable.

When I was little, writing things for school, I assumed I had to accept whatever words came into my head: those were the words I would write down for the teacher. That is, my writing mode was passive. Concomitant was the feeling that whatever I said in a poem or essay had to express what I "really" felt. In other words, I had almost no control over the entire process.

Ron Padgett describes not just a childhood experience of writing but also what it's like to write a first draft. As so many writers say, "The story wrote itself."

How wonderful! But such a draft seems immutable and leaves the writer powerless. The more we write, the more we understand exactly how malleable these *things* are. As the poet Chase Twichell writes,

> It's hard to remember, when you're struggling with the words in front of you, that those words found their way onto the paper fairly arbitrarily. That is, you'd certainly have written a different version of the poem had you sat down to work in the afternoon instead of in the morning. Cutting a poem apart is a way of making holes in it, windows, a way of keeping it open for a while, so that you can enlarge and refine your sense of it while it's still rough.

Scissors keep Twichell involved in her creation. They open her poems to possibilities; they help her play, reorganize, deepen her thought, broaden her associations. In what she calls "the violence of reimagining," she continues creative play beyond drafting. Rather than let the first version dictate what's possible, she seizes her authority as a writer and flings wide the windows.

Pennebaker and Janel Seagal note that "writing helps people to 'reorganize' their thoughts and feelings about . . . experiences, thus creating 'coherence' and/or 'story' and 'meaning.'" Healing—the *aha!* of discovery—comes not just from disclosing memories; it also comes from "reconnecting with and expressing the 'felt, bodily' aspects of these experiences and being able to relinquish any unhelpful or inappropriate 'autobiographical' narratives of the experience that may have been learned or imposed." This rearranging of experience and the formation of a functioning philosophy also happen as we write fiction. "We stand back, weigh things as we do not have time to do in life; and the effect of great fiction is to temper real experience, modify prejudice, humanize," John Gardner says. "By imitating we come to understand the thing we imitate."

While we may feel great release upon drafting stories, we are significantly changed when we reorganize these narratives for coherence and beauty. We develop our reflective capacity and increase our self-understanding. We add layers until the story contains a complexity and depth of which our ordinary consciousness is incapable. The creation of a thing simultaneously *of* the self and *beyond* the self is an extraordinary, mighty, and mysterious act. This, I believe, is why Carol Bly calls revision the holy work of making literature.

When we write a story, just as when we tell a therapist a memory, the process becomes an event in its own right. We do not simply relate what's happened; the telling itself has ramifications. In this sense, the page is alive. Writing gives our thoughts, imaginings, feelings, and memories form. Their power over us diminishes, instead entering our being as new self-awareness, and it enters our text in its capacity to move others. As William Stafford writes to his fellow poets, "The moon you are describing is the one you are creating. From the very beginning of your utterance you are creating your own authority." Art is a form of public testimony, and this context (unlike private therapy) yields different internal transformations. Art teaches us the potential influence of a single voice within a vast conversation; it invites us to participate beyond the private sphere. The moon we create shines on other people.

By creating a *thing* out of a feeling, idea, or memory, whether a piece of fiction, nonfiction, or poetry, we also distance the self from the text. The feeling, idea, or memory is no longer insubstantial; it's something we can shape. If, then, we revise our text, a remarkable transformation begins. We make thousands of choices about how to tell the story—the order, the pacing, when to reflect and when to describe, which themes to pull forward and which to relinquish. We connect emotions to events, we grow aware of hidden motivations, we uncover a unifying frame. We manifest our principles and worldviews within a specific, crafted form. We take responsibility as constructors of our content. "One sheds one's sicknesses in books," D. H. Lawrence writes, "repeats and presents again one's emotions, to be master of them." **By making choices about how we represent the events that formed us or the ideas that have come to us, we gain creative authority—we become authors.**[3]

For writers of memoir and autobiographical fiction, claiming authority over one's memories is the hardest part of revision. We can flesh out scenes, add dialogue, pay attention to character development; we can fiddle with craft and make worthwhile changes. But at some point, all autobiographical writers must seriously consider revising their content. Revision is not simply about evaluating and changing the *form* of our writing; it's also about adding layers of understanding to the *content*. And when our content is our lives, this means undertaking serious emotional work.

---

3   Some people define writers as those who write and authors as those who have published. I don't. Writers are those who write, yes, but authors are those who make intentional choices about their craft and content. They've gained authority over their material.

Many students quit here. The demands of the craft have implications larger than they expected. The version of their experiences they wanted to write proves false, shallow, or incomplete. Before their work can successfully address a reader, they must call this version into question, asking themselves if there aren't other ways of telling the story, other insights into what happened, and more emotional nuance than they've allowed. They must unearth the lies they've lived with and dig deeper.

Lest fiction writers think they're off the hook, the same inner work is required for psychologically accurate and emotionally textured fiction. The goal of mapping out narratives, Peter Turchi says, "is to recognize unconscious constraints so that we can make conscious choices." The fiction writer's unconscious constraints are just as rigid as the memoirist's; they define the boundaries of their characters' actions, range of emotions, and relational possibilities; they determine the extent of a created world's believability; they are governed by the author's cosmology. When students of mine leave memoir for the "safer" medium of fiction, I laugh. They may no longer pull skeletons out of family closets, but fiction still exposes the workings of the subconscious, dark secrets, and hidden obsessions. When fiction writers draw from life experiences, they must unhook themselves from "what really happened." The story needs space to find its own truth.

Gaining authority over your material demands *research*. Deep in revision, this research is emotional. Where is the truth of your story? Why are you affected by this truth? How? Where does this truth reside, or need to reside, in the wider world? If your pursuit of answers to these questions requires your going into therapy, go. If your pursuit requires journaling or taking a retreat or having hard conversations with your family, or any action within or away from your writing that helps you examine your story with fearless eyes, do it. You can't author a book without becoming an authority on the emotional core of your story.

At the root of the word *author* is the Middle English word for "increase." We become authors by expanding the depth and breadth of our work. Authors take creative ownership of their content; they wield their power to shape stories. This deliberate shaping is how human beings make meaning. Revision is how we exercise our spiritual, meaning-making, purpose-seeking muscles.

Paradoxically, once we begin exercising this power, we feel pushback. That's the story asserting its will. This pushback and our willingness to heed it invite us into relationship with a bigger consciousness unfolding in the creative process. **We come into our authorship when we become co-creators**. The interplay between the ego's magnificent drive and utter surrender to the story's will is the alchemy that fuels transformation—of the text and of the writer's heart.

Exercises

Emotional Research

- *What is the primary emotion behind your story? Explore its origins. What memories do you associate with this emotion? Where does your imagination take you when you contemplate this emotion?*

- *What is one central question or idea behind your story? Explore the origin of this question or idea.*

- *What part of your story do you tend to avoid? Go there. If you're writing fiction, have your character experience a dream, deliver a soliloquy, or indulge in a fantasy. If you're writing nonfiction, introduce difficult material by admitting you don't want to disclose it, then disclose it ("What I don't want to tell you is . . ."). Or contradict yourself ("Sure I loved her, but I also hated her"). Or catch yourself lying ("What I just said isn't true. Really . . .").*

- *Imagine for a minute that you can't write this story. What would be the consequences of repressing this creative act? Write out this scenario. Then reflect: What do these imagined consequences reveal about your need to write?*

Emotional Authority

When I read a new client's manuscript, one of the questions I ask myself is, "With what authority is the writer writing?" I'm not looking for professional expertise or a knowledge base or a position of power. I'm looking for wisdom. Every one of us is an authority on some aspect of living. The woman who was pimped by her parents when she was a child is an authority on betrayal; the priest who drinks in private is an authority on secrecy; the frazzled mother of young children is an authority on mundane love.

Our books usually center on some aspect of our emotional authority. What emotional authority does your story explore? How might you claim that authority more fully? What might this authority reveal about your book's heartbeat?

Detachment

So: The writer's original state of overidentification with the story is good and necessary for a first draft. We *want* to pour our blood and being onto the page. We *want* a headlong dash through the imagination. But writers interested in developing their work must eventually transition from feeling like their stories are an extension of self—an extra limb—to external and independent beings. In creative nonfiction, writers working toward authorship move from a private, journal-like record where the I on the page *is* the author to a text that engages others and the I is a character or narrator. In fiction, writers working toward authorship create characters who are people in their own right, making choices in keeping with *their* personalities rather than the author's and functioning in a world with its own inherent rules. A writer must practice detachment to create art.

Consider child-rearing, an even more prolonged and difficult creative process. The overidentification between parent and newborn fades as the child grows; we *want* our school-aged child to venture out and run back into our arms; we *want* our adult child to be independent with a unique and separate personality. Your first draft is your baby. Revision raises that baby; gradually you wean it from your sense of identity; you step away as it learns to walk; you let it make mistakes. Moderated, increasing detachment is the most loving and skillful way to develop our work.

Our job is to serve the story as it grows, heeding its various and changing needs.

Making Deliberate Choices

Eventually writers recognize how unformed a first draft is. Its length, voice, structure, and even genre are not inevitable; they are each one of many possibilities. Authoring means accepting bursts of inspiration *and* making deliberate choices. Both are creative. Both are empowering.

Betsy Lerner, agent and editor, rants eloquently on the subject of writers making choices:

> Though the writer's aim is to convey truth, it certainly isn't to tell the truth per se. There is simply nothing worse than a novice writer who cries out in his own defense, when a scene is criticized for not seeming real, that "it really happened that way." No, no, no. Everything you put on the page is a deliberate manipulation of what happened, written to keep the reader entertained, moved, sympathetic, horrified, scared, whatever. You are never writing what really happened. Instead, you are choosing words, building images, creating a rhythm, sense, and structure through which to move your characters and unfold your story. You are making a thousand minuscule choices that you hope will add up in such a way that your readers believe what they're reading is real. And this is why, when the writer is successful, the best fiction reads like nonfiction and the best nonfiction like a novel.

My students usually bristle at the word *manipulation*; they are straightforward, honest Midwesterners. But when Lerner says we're never writing what really happened, she means this literally—we can't re-create life. Words are not flesh. Just as a map is a two-dimensional representation of a landscape, a written story is a two-dimensional representation of human experience. It's a created thing. We can't hit the "play" button of our memory or imagination, take notes, and expect literature. Facts don't make a story. The translation from three-dimensional life to two-dimensional representation requires effort—craft, that is, or "a deliberate manipulation of what happened."

The events we've experienced as memoirists or imagined as fiction writers are inconsequential. What matters is what we make of these events, what purpose they serve. I remember a high school student's story about a cashier at the grocery checkout asking him, "Paper or plastic?" His ensuing internal moral conundrum, played out over pages, was hilarious. This student had transformed a mundane moment into artistic social commentary. He'd made a story.

Rather than being daunted by the thousand miniscule decisions pending in revision, look at it this way: The playing field is wide open. Let the fun begin! Here you can deliberately shape your story, which is also a way of shaping the world.

Hospitality

We writers must be adept at both dismissing the audience for the sake of creating a safe, private space and warmly welcoming the audience into the world we've created. What a paradox! If we write solely for ourselves, our work becomes solipsistic and sloppy. Our minds, however bright, are only so big; our lives, however expansive, are limited. This is why unedited journals are rarely published;

there's too much shlock. If we remain in the cloud of privacy, we not only betray our intention to communicate with others; we also deprive our work of the great broadening an audience requires.

Consideration of audience is absolutely necessary to the development of creative work. **Art is essentially dialogue**—between the artist and the source of creativity, between the artist and audience, between the artist and artists who have come before, between the artist and society. Awareness of these conversations helps writers find the universal elements of their narratives and launch them beyond the private sphere. By setting our work within historical moments, social movements, religious thought, psychological currents, and other broad contexts, we link the smallness of our memories or imagined worlds to that web of commonality that connects humanity. We remove ourselves from isolation. We participate in community.

Whether or not a literal audience ever reads our writing—whether or not this is something we want—we can incorporate these conversational gifts into our writing process.

Craft is a form of hospitality. When readers (real or imagined) show up at your door, how do you invite them in? What makes them comfortable but not too comfortable? What nourishment or conversation might make them linger? When they leave, what will they take with them? The secret to hospitality, I learned when working in retreat ministry, is not good housekeeping, not good interior decorating, not even good food or programming. These external expressions of welcome are important but only work when they are actual extensions of the host's heart. Nothing puts a guest more at ease than the host's own ease; nothing calls a guest forward like the host's attention.

The locus of hospitality in literature lies within the author's heart. A heart that practices confidence, curiosity, and self-awareness—qualities fostered by writing for no audience—welcomes readers. A writer's hospitality is what is meant by that slippery term *voice*. We usually think of voice as an expression of personality, but it's more dynamic than that. A strong voice is relational; it invites the reader into our sensibilities, our sense of order, and our values, while also acknowledging human difference. Even an unreliable narrator's voice is undergirded by a steady, hospitable, authorial presence.

Another lesson I learned in retreat ministry is that every significant spiritual journey at some point arrives back in community. Deep listening requires time apart from daily routines, but then any new life that emerges in solitude needs the touchstones of work, relationship, and society to gain meaning and relevance. Mystics of every tradition agree—the effectiveness of prayer or meditation is evident in the actions that follow. Contemplation gains traction in action.

Likewise with creative practice; the craft of writing is a rigorous discipline through which we open our inner life to another, or to the Other. What's born in privacy gains texture and merit by becoming accessible. Readers are our crucible. Awareness of the writer's role in culture making helps us participate in a broader experience of creativity. This is essentially what revision is about—seeing our material again with an eye open to these widening circles of connection.

I believe the best time to welcome the audience into most creative projects is after the second or third draft, once we've searched for the heart of our work and risked exposing some truth. As we move through drafts, we can begin to ask questions that open our story to others:

- Who are my readers and why might they care?

- How might I hook my readers' attention and raise the stakes?

- Have I thoroughly introduced my characters, my setting, my questions?

- How might I make my experience or my characters' experience available to readers so they are participants in my story rather than observers?

- Am I *showing* my ideas by grounding them in scenes?

- What in my story touches the common human experience?

In a demanding return to the "So what?" question, we answer this time with hospitality. Now that we've found content that matters, we shape it to interact with others.

Publishing as a Bridge

In the minds of most writers, the idea of an audience gets tangled with publishing. I suggest separating the two. Your audience is not a publisher.

The publishing industry is profit-driven; it attempts, often unsuccessfully, to anticipate the desires of paying readers. We all know gifted authors who have received scores of rejections. We've all read best-selling books that were crap. With some exceptions, publishers don't see their missions as fostering civic discourse or supporting literary innovation or nurturing the intellectual life of our country. They want money. When writers use acceptance by a publisher as a measure of success, they give the publishing industry too much power.

A publisher's willingness to print your work is only one measure of its worth. Healthy writers lean on multiple measures: the satisfaction you get from the writing process, the impact your work has on individual readers' lives, the conversations that arise between people because of your work, and readers' long-term relationship with your work. What brings life and light into your heart and community? A more reliable measure of your art's value is the aliveness that springs from others' receptive, creative engagement with it.

Besides, the publishing industry is now in flux as e-books, self-publishing, and the Internet change readers' access to text. What used to be an institutional filter for printed material has splintered into thousands of venues that bring particular content to particular audiences. The dictums of the industry no longer stand. Chances are good that your need to write a story can now be matched with a reader's need to read it.

As wonderfully democratic as this is, a word of caution: Self-publishing makes it unreasonably easy for amateur writers to cave in to their resistance to revision and shortchange a book's development.

I suggest delaying thoughts of publishing until late in the writing process.[4] When a hypothetical editor or *The New York Times Book Review* or a supersensitive family member enters a writer's mind, the

---

4   The exception is when the venue is part of your motivation for writing, as is usually the case in journalism. I think it's healthiest for literary writers who must consider the requirements of the publication—word count, style, audience, and so forth—to also dismiss these constrictions in favor of absolute freedom. As soon as a potential venue limits rather than fosters exploration, publishing no longer serves our work. Think of publication requirements like the rules of a sonnet; the boundaries of the form can either straightjacket or enliven your content.

likelihood of writer's block increases exponentially. Remember that exploration, play, and truth telling can result in stories that move the human heart in ways seeking affirmation never can. Better to consider your readers real people with ragged, hungry lives. Better to envision writing for your younger self or your imaginary friend or your neighbors or book group or a lonely Montana rancher who asks the same existential questions you do when gazing at the night sky. Publication is just a bridge to connect your inner world with another's.

Exercises

Your Ideal Reader

When my sister was in grade school, she and her best friend made a pact: They would write their diaries to each other. My sister never actually shared what she wrote with her friend, but conceiving of this friend as her diary's audience made her eager to write.

Consider applying this idea to your creative work. If you can conceptualize the most intimate, curious, forgiving audience for your writing, this orientation will affect what and how you write.

Write a character sketch of your ideal reader. What is her personality? What motivates him? What does she need? Why is he reading your story?

Letter to Your Reader

Write a "dear reader" letter. How do you hope to connect with your reader? What do you hope your reader takes away from your work? Why?

Your Broad Audience

Francine Prose suggests asking, "Who is listening?" Explore many answers in your notebook. Who is your broader audience? What aspect or subgroup of humanity are you addressing? Who holds you accountable? What kinds of emotions, memories, or thoughts do you hope to ignite within your readers?

For the Love of It

The ultimate answer to the "So what?" question is "For the love of it." **Love is the essential ingredient in making literature**. If you are concerned with the quality of your writing, if you're striving for publication or recognition, you may think this sounds sentimental. But listen to David Foster Wallace:

> There's something kind of timelessly vital and sacred about good writing. This thing doesn't have that much to do with talent. . . . Talent's just an instrument. It's like having a pen that works instead of one that doesn't. . . . It seems like the big distinction between good art and so-so art lies somewhere in the art's heart's purpose, the agenda of the consciousness behind the text. It's got something to do with love. With having the discipline to talk out of the part of yourself that can love instead of the part that just wants to be loved. . . . It seems like one of the things really great fiction-writers do . . . is "give" the reader something. The reader walks away from the real art heavier than she came into it. Fuller. All the attention and engagement and work you need

to get from the reader can't be for your benefit; it's got to be for hers. What's poisonous about the cultural environment today is that it makes this so scary to try to carry out. Really good work probably comes out of a willingness to disclose yourself, open yourself up in spiritual and emotional ways that risk making you really feel something. To be willing to sort of die in order to move the reader, somehow. Even now I'm scared about how sappy this'll look in print, saying this. And the effort actually to do it, not just talk about it, requires a kind of courage I don't seem to have yet.

John Gardner concurs: "Great art celebrates life's potential, offering a vision unmistakably and unsentimentally rooted in love." These men speak in the context of a cultural insistence that accomplishment is attributable to talent, effort, or intelligence—qualities we can quantify. Love, on the other hand, is an eternal mystery. We don't know precisely how love works, especially within the act of creation.

Nonetheless, I believe that if we can write from a place of love—for the subject matter, for the writing process, for the language, for our readers—then we're on the right path. The practice of exercising love brings us joy. It changes us, always for the better. Love requires tending, which in art-making means learning about our subject, building our skills, staying faithful to our projects, and working hard. The effort of loving through craft makes literature. **If we fall short of making art or if we make art that no one sees or understands, the world is still unquestionably better. The exercise of love is never wasted**.

CHAPTER FIVE

Deep Listening

Jim was a thoughtful, retired pastor who came to me for writing support. Because he had been confined to a wheelchair since his twenties, a wound had formed at his sacrum that proved difficult to heal and challenged his faith. Jim wrote personal essays about his struggle to understand his affliction while enduring multiple surgeries and long periods of immobility.

Then his project stalled. Jim had expected the wound to close and provide neat closure to his essays. When the wound didn't heal, Jim couldn't finish his project.

I told Jim (rather insensitively) that a physical healing would be a clichéd ending to his story. Besides, his essays weren't about the wound so much as the questions the wound posed for him. The wound didn't need resolution for his writing to be complete, but his questions did. Or at least they needed discussion and movement. Maybe learning to live with lack of closure *was* the resolution to his essays.

When he took time to reflect, Jim realized that his wound forced him to be open in ways that strengthened his listening skills. It made him dependent on others' care, keeping him humble. Even as he railed against the limitations imposed by the wound and sought medical solutions, he came to understand himself as a wounded healer, working from a place of vulnerability. Jim wrote his way into acceptance—and, in the process, learned to love revision. His completed essays awed me, not because the writing was fabulous (it was forthright and plain), but because it was true.

Writers have the potential to discover wisdom beyond what we currently embody. "Great novels are always a little more intelligent than their authors," says Milan Kundera. Encountering this intelligence in our work stretches us, opens us.

A story has a hidden life—a soul, if you will. How writers nourish this soul significantly affects our work and our well-being. This tending is really active listening. It's both willful, sprung from the self, and responsive, heeding that life force beyond the story and its readers. We can bring our smaller, circumscribed ideas into humble conversation with the wider possibilities of the page. This is the same gesture the Christian mystics call surrender and Zen Buddhists call letting go, a releasing of the limited self in service of . . . nothing, everything, Mystery, the Other. "There comes a time in the composition of a work of fiction," Alice McDermott writes, "when the writer must put aside all plans and intentions and preconceived notions of the work at hand and simply proceed, blindly, if you will, with the writing itself." You know the most effective craft techniques and the rules of grammar; you have refined your skills; you can recognize quality, *and* you disregard all that to set your heart on what matters. This letting go is the most difficult aspect of craft for writers to learn and is the writer's form of faith. "We must teach ourselves," as Seamus Heaney says, "to walk on air against our better judgment."

In revision, we probe the many ways in which our stories are not our selves. They have their own integrity, their own identity.

We can have broken, conflicted lives and still write honest, complete, unified memoir. We can create functioning fictional families while our own falls apart. "Poetry cannot say the unsayable. It builds something that holds the unsayable," poet Marie Howe says. Our interaction with this container has tangible consequences, in our prose and in our psyches. **Writing is redemptive. It grants us an experience of wholeness in an otherwise fractured world**.

What Is Your Story Asking?

A story has a life force, an inner fire, all its own. The writer's task is to stoke that fire until it roars.

We know stories have their own wills; that's why writing is fun. You might rant angrily in your journal but then, as the pages pass, grow calm and aware. Or you intend to record one memory but then veer into perplexing, unremembered territory. Or your pre-planned plot gets upended by a wayward character. In her essay "Memory and Imagination," Patricia Hampl reflects on an early draft of a memory of a piano lesson. "The piece hasn't yet found its subject; it isn't yet about what it wants to be about. Note: What IT wants, not what I want." Isn't this why we write? We love being pushed and pulled by a story. We cherish those moments when, as Ray Bradbury puts it, truths leap "out of bushes like quail before gunshot." We write for the surprise.

But writing is also unsettling: We're not entirely in charge. A force rises up from the page. It pushes back. It has an agenda.

When we put our hearts into our work—when we write material we genuinely care about with curiosity, initially disregarding what others will think—writing is a dialogue between self and subject. As we compose, we're surprised by the material that shows up. As we revise, we're surprised by the story's slow disclosure of its inner life.

The poet Michael Dennis Browne calls this life "the poem behind the poem." This "is the one we usually fail to imagine, the one that fails to get written; the poem must always surprise its writer, both in its particulars and in its overall enterprise, coming as it does unbidden from the pen." Unlike the outer story that motivates us to begin, the inner story—the movement of its soul—is unearthed as we contemplate, allow time to pass, and revise.

Revision is a call and response between the writer's intent and the story's soul. The writer needs a plan to begin this dialogue ("I'm writing about X"). But the writer also needs to step back to see what has appeared on the page. "It is not uncommon for me to be six or seven full drafts into an essay before I realize, 'Aha, that's what this essay is going to be about,'" writes Dinty Moore. Creative work happens in dynamic relationship with a subject. Half of our work is generative—inventing, expressing, reflecting, shaping. The other half is responsive. We listen for the life welling up and shift our efforts to support it. We ask: What is this piece *really* about? What might it want to become? What truth is asking to be told? What pumps energy into this creation and how can I, its author, amplify that pumping?

So I shout out a version of my story. Then there's a pause, during which I ponder, reread, note the surprises, ask my colleagues for their thoughts, discuss the subject matter with my spouse—that is, listen for what the story wants. The draft always responds with a nudge—*go here*. Perhaps I'm in conversation not only with loved ones and colleagues but with my subconscious self or with the collective unconscious or with God.

Does this sound too mystical? Here's Meredith Sue Willis's more down-to-earth depiction:

The best creative writing . . . comes out of a process of moving constantly in new directions, deeper directions. Ideally, such writing works through a dialectical process: it is irrational and spontaneous for a while, then rational and planned. You are gripped by some idea or image, which you draft in the heat of inspiration. Later, in the cool light of reason, you cut, reorganize, and add what you perceive to be missing. Then something in what you've written gives you a new idea, and you draft rapidly again, making new connections, perhaps coming up with something you never meant to include. Then you follow with another "rational" session, or show it to another person. Finally, ideally, after many rounds of this process of thesis and antithesis, there is a synthesis, at which point a leap to something that is greater than the sum of its parts becomes possible.

"Step by step the wonder of unexpected supply keeps growing," Robert Frost writes. **Mystery is limitless. Revision helps us harvest it, bit by bit**.

Exercise

What the Story Wants

During the drafting and revising of a project, periodically explore the possibility that your writing is asking something of you. What might want to be written now?

Toolbox: Questions

*Be patient toward all that is unsolved in your heart.
. . . Try to love the questions themselves like locked
rooms and like books that are written in a foreign
tongue. Do not now seek the answers which cannot
be given you because you would not be able to live
them. And the point is, live everything. Live the questions now. Perhaps you will then gradually, without noticing it, live along some distant day into the
answer.*

That Rainer Maria Rilke's *Letters to a Young Poet* is
quoted more often to spiritual seekers than to writers strikes
me as strange. Questions are a writer's best tools. They pry
open possibility. They expose alternatives. They deepen and
broaden our material's scope. They ask that we see through
new eyes. They motivate. They open us to love.

When writers are genuinely curious about a subject, we
naturally ask questions. What history informs the moment
you described? Did you or your character feel just one way,
or were there contradictory feelings? What motivates this
character? When I bring a piece for my writing group to
discuss, they don't respond with a critique; they engage in a
freewheeling inquiry. Questions are addressed to the piece
itself, not to me as the author, so everyone can speculate
about answers. After the meeting, I continue these invigorating discussions in my project journal. I want to prolong
the fun.

Carl Jung suggests that, rather than analyze dreams, we "dream the dream onward." Questions—addressed with others or in the privacy of a notebook—help us dream the story onward. My colleague Mary Carroll Moore calls questions that unlock new material "gateway questions." When we live and love questions rather than striving for answers, we pass through a gate into our story's expansive potential.

Of the hundreds of questions generated by any creative exploration, one usually rises to the top. Pivotal, unanswerable, it drives both you and your piece. This is your story's heartbeat. Finding this question is perhaps the most rewarding moment of every project.

Questions form a bridge between our innermost being and our written work. Loving the questions keeps us humble, seeking, and open. When we love the questions, we orient our hearts toward process rather than outcome—the essential work of any contemplative practice.

Exercises

Content Questions

Consider a draft you're currently working on. List at least ten questions you have, not about the crafting of the piece but about its content; questions such as: What was I feeling in this scene? Why did my character make this decision? What history led to this moment? In other words, what don't you yet know about the material? Choose one question and write a response.

Life Questions

What are the three central questions of your life? Don't dismiss this exercise as impossible; just suppose that there are only three and write them down. Then ask yourself which question your current writing project addresses. How? Why? How might the project better illuminate your question?

Toolbox: Generating in Revision

I recently led a manuscript review for a second draft of a book-length memoir. The class discussed what the book was about, helped the author articulate its purpose and drive, and named the thematic threads that unified its many disparate anecdotes. Some of these themes surprised the author; most confirmed her intentions or instincts; all needed development. The class wanted *more*: more reflection, more illustrative examples, more links between the narrative and the various questions the narrative raised. The manuscript was already a good 250-plus pages, so I wasn't surprised when the author cornered me after class and asked, "How can I make these changes without the book getting huge?"

Almost every manuscript goes through this stage. The author has plenty of material. Individual chapters or scenes are complete but not yet cohesive. The outer story—the plot—travels across the book, but the inner ideas or questions—the themes—are ragged and shallow. Or vice versa—the ideas are great but not grounded in story. The book needs both a driving purpose and a grounding plot, which means another revision, one that requires the author to think and feel across the entire manuscript.

But how? The obvious and sometimes frustrating answer is: The writer needs to write more. Students critiquing each other's work frequently ask for "More, more, more!" The suggestion implies that readers want more length, when in fact what they need is depth.

Ironically, adding depth to our work requires generating more pages. Writing works backward: We write to discover what we're trying to say. During revision, we depart from the boundaries of a draft to find new material. We identify pivotal places in the narrative and excavate what lies beneath. We can then choose which of this new material will enhance the story, and include it.

First, it's good to generate writing *outside* the project in a revision journal:

- Why am I writing this? What's in it—especially in the writing process and in the subject matter—for me?

- How do I feel about my draft? Where are my places of discomfort? What am I attached to and why?

- What might this draft be asking of me? What might it want to become?

- Where do I feel stuck in this project? Why?

- Where do I feel ease and flow in this project? Why?

Second, practice any activity that gives you greater access to your subconscious.

- Daydream; let your mind wander in response to your draft, then record where it goes. Brenda Ueland found that four-mile walks helped unlock her work. Some writers draw, do needlepoint, or gaze out the window. Many take long road trips.

- Create character sketches for the players in your story. What are their core motivations? Why?

- Play with musical theater. What's your character's theme song? What's the soundtrack behind each scene?

- Draw scenes from or abstract images that evoke your story, or create a collage to convey your story's movement or essence.

Third, find the rabbit holes in your manuscript—those tunnels into mysterious, often interior worlds you've yet to investigate. Here are some places where writers commonly camouflage or neglect the inner story:

- Those spots where you *tell* (use summary, reflective writing, or exposition) rather than *show* (use scene). Are there details or scenes that might do this work more effectively for the reader? Pay attention to the symbolism of these details or scenes.

- Turning points. Have you done moments of change in the narrative justice? Do you use sensory details? Are the inner lives of characters apparent to the reader? Are all the symbolic nuances of the moment illuminated?

- Scenes that set down the emotional roots of your story. Have you given the reader the history necessary to make sense of the characters' motivations? Is the context thoroughly established?

- Scenes you have avoided because they demand difficult emotional work. Write them.

- Passages toward which you feel unreasonable resistance. Dig in.

- Consequences of the action. Is there a moment that illuminates how your character has been affected by this story?

- Reflection. If your piece has a narrator, has the narrator reflected on the story? What's the relationship between the narrator and the narrative?

- Stake. From the opening sentence, is there a strong sense that something important is at stake—for the character, for the author, and for the reader?

Notice how these questions focus on filling in gaps and heightening tension—tasks that are nearly impossible in a first draft. Philip Lopate describes the personal essayist as attempting "to surround a something—a subject, a mood, a problematic irritation—by coming at it from all angles, wheeling and diving like a hawk, each seemingly digressive spiral actually taking us closer to the heart of the matter." This is also a good description of generating in revision. Coming at our story from only one angle makes a one-dimensional story; coming at it again and again, fleshing out memories, complicating characters, questioning motives, and layering awareness upon fresh awareness create a multifaceted and gripping story. "To make anything interesting," writes Gustave Flaubert, "you simply have to look at it long enough."

Generating in response to a draft is a form of listening. We listen in the cracks; we listen underneath the words. Many writers get nervous about the scattered nature of this kind of generating. New scenes upset the apple cart; they don't fit within a sequential first draft. But this is exactly what we're after in revision. We want to drive wedges of fresh light into old prose. We heed what the story wants rather than our own tidy, limited agenda.

Exercises

The Unwritten Part

In the center of a blank sheet of paper, draw a circle and write inside what you believe your piece is about. (See the illustration below.) In a ring encompassing this circle, note the contents of your current draft—events, reflections, anecdotes. Then draw another ring encompassing both. Here make note of other material that is part of your story but not in your draft. Ask: What material is unwritten but relevant? What more might this be about? What does this story remind me of? What else do I think about this topic? What questions arise? What history undergirds the story? What future events will reveal the consequences of this story?

Then choose one fresh idea and begin writing, not worrying where it will fit into your piece.

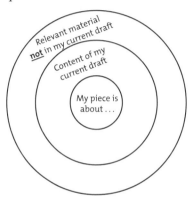

Expansion and Contraction

For this exercise, I suggest choosing a short piece (under ten pages) or a small section of a longer piece. As you work through these steps, don't rework the previous draft. Start afresh, keeping your muscles limber and your mind open.

Step 1: Rewrite your draft, doubling its length. Don't just add more events to the narrative; rather, deepen the events and reflections that are already there. Add more details. Reveal more emotions. If you are writing in first person, allow your narrator to reflect more. (If your first draft was six pages, this draft should be twelve.)

Step 2: Rewrite again, this time halving your original length. In this revision, try to get at the essence of the piece. What idea or emotion is absolutely necessary to these pages? Which details are crucial? Get your piece down to its barest, most beautiful elements. (If your first draft was six pages, this draft should be three.)

Step 3: Scan your step one draft for elements that bring your story or ideas to life. Allow your step two draft to teach you about your piece's heartbeat. Now, rewrite a third time, incorporating these elements into a fresh version that returns your piece to its original length.

If you're committed to learning revision, I recommend that you take a piece through these steps at least once. Done with an open heart, this exercise teaches revision's fundamentals. Expansion allows a piece to breathe and deepen. Contraction compresses, accelerates, and focuses. Combined, these elements benefit your final product.

Toolbox: Listening to the Details

Beginning writers assume that details bore. Experienced writers know that details *speak*. A story's soul hides in the details. Details can imbue a scene with significance.

The challenge is to find the right sensory, suggestive details. These carry weight—they work for the story's heartbeat, they reveal emotion, they move the plot forward. When we enter our pivotal scenes and take a good look around, we always find such hardworking details. For example, in Laura Flynn's beautiful San Francisco memoir, *Swallow the Ocean*, she describes a tense dinner scene where symptoms of her mother's schizophrenia begin to appear. Conversation is awkward; Flynn's mother is paranoid about her husband's business colleague.

> My father swallowed hard. "Sally, you don't know him," he said.
>
> "I don't need to know him," she said slowly. "I know."
>
> I arranged my peas across my plate with my fork. The fork was heavy in my hand, weighty silver, but dull and tarnished. The peas were a vivid green against the white plate. They rolled and bounced as I moved them. The almost perfect spheres created patterns on the plate, choosing a twin, forming a triad, then shifting alignments again. . . .
>
> I pushed a few peas onto my knife, and glanced back up at my mother, trying to catch her eye. This was a cue for her, an old familiar one. I wanted her to smile and recite for me, "I eat my peas with honey. I've done it all my life. It makes my peas taste funny, but it keeps them on my knife." She didn't move.
>
> "Sally, can't we just finish eating our dinner?" my father said, still making a great show of eating his own steak.

Note how much work the details accomplish. The silverware is expensive but neglected. The child is overly attentive to her peas, evidence that she's staring at her plate to avoid the tension between her parents. What happens on the surface isn't nearly as important as the emotional dynamics underneath—the subtext. The details, and not abstract pronouncements, point to the story's heartbeat: Laura's beloved mother, the one who recites rhymes about peas, will be consumed by paranoia.

Often we don't recognize the telling details. A student of mine wrote about how education had liberated him from a tough, working class childhood. Early in the piece he'd written some anecdotes about his family home, including one of flying a kite inside a fenced-in yard; he told our class he planned to cut it since it seemed irrelevant. But the class noted the scene's beautiful symbolism—the kite rising above the confined perimeters of his yard much as he, through education, had gained perspective and a means of escape. He was amazed. The details illuminated his story's heartbeat.

Artifacts, sensory experiences, elements of setting—the seemingly superficial components of stories—are loaded with potential meaning. God, as they say, is in the details. Carl Jung asserts that the imagination's work is to "grasp the inner facts and portray them in images true to their nature." This incarnational work, the joining of physical detail and inner import, is the writer's magic.

We locate the life-giving dimension of our story by lingering, expanding, and turning over details for layers of symbolism. Early on in revision, we can revisit our story's important scenes to ask what in their external details reveals the emotional or relational dynamics of each moment. What resonates?

Once you identify heavy-lifting details, lean into them. On the page, length communicates significance. Take this example, from early in Paula Fox's novel *Desperate Characters*:

> The cat had begun to clean its whiskers. Sophie caressed its back again, drawing her fingers along until they met the sharp furry crook where the tail turned up. The cat's back rose convulsively to press against her hand. She smiled, wondering how often, if ever before, the cat had felt a friendly human touch, and she was still smiling as the cat reared up on its hind legs, even as it struck her with extended claws, smiling right up to that second when it sank its teeth into the back of her left hand and hung from her flesh so that she nearly fell forward, stunned and horrified, yet conscious enough of Otto's presence to smother the cry that arose in her throat as she jerked her hand back from that circle of barbed wire. She pushed out with her other hand, and as the sweat broke out on her forehead, as her flesh crawled and tightened, she said, "No, no, stop that!" to the cat, as if it had done nothing more than beg for food, and in the midst of her pain and dismay she was astonished to hear how cool her voice was. Then, all at once, the claws released her and flew back as though to deliver another blow, but then the cat turned—it seemed in mid-air—

and sprang from the porch, disappearing into the shadowed yard below.

Note how the cat's movements and Sophie's reactions hint at difficulties between Sophie and Otto; they expose Sophie's ideals and insincerity; they point to a suppressed violence that plagues the couple. Every detail is working hard.

Length signifies emotional importance. But the inverse is more instructive: The more emotionally important a moment is, the longer a writer should linger. Spend time with your telling details. Details that *do work* are always gripping, no matter how many or how intricate. Flannery O'Connor puts it this way:

> The novelist makes his statements by selection, and if he is any good, he selects every word for a reason, every detail for a reason, every incident for a reason, and arranges them in a certain time-sequence for a reason. . . . Detail has to be controlled by some overall purpose, and every detail has to be put to work for you. Art is selective. What is there is essential and creates movement.

Remember that purpose is both discovered and intended. Details plus purpose equal movement.

Exercises

The Mind's Eye

When working on a significant scene, pause. Close your eyes. Imagine yourself in that place and moment. What do you smell? See? Hear? Allow your subconscious to draw you to small details. Pay particular attention to anything that bears emotional weight. Note these details in your project journal first, where you have freedom to explore them without concern for disrupting the draft.

Generating Details

Choose a scene, then generate lists of as many details as you can within that scene. Give a column to the objects that are present. Give a column to each of the senses. Then scan your lists for telling details that might reveal your scene's inner life. Incorporate them into the draft.

Details Carry Weight

Identify one scene that's absolutely critical to your story. Expand it. Let it breathe. Write it in as much detail as you can, using all the senses. Be sure to include the setting. What's happening to your character's body? Emotions? Thoughts? Then journal: Why, exactly, is this scene so important? What's obvious about its importance and what is not so obvious?

Now identify some part of your project about which you're ambivalent. Perhaps it doesn't belong; perhaps it belongs but is lackluster. Journal: What work is this section doing? What work isn't it doing? How might it do this work? Should it be tightened, expanded, re-worked, or cut?

Dialogue with an Image

Choose an image from your draft (an object, a view, a freeze-frame from a scene) that has energy for you. Set a timer for ten minutes. Writing quickly, without thinking, dialogue with this image. Allow it to speak in its own voice. Ask it what it wants. Allow it to ask questions. Afterward, ask, "If this image had its say, what would my piece be about?"

Stretching the Moment

In a scene or draft, locate the following:

- *turning points in the story or progression of ideas*

- *character introductions*

- *the setting*

- *introductions of conflicts*

- *moments when conflicts escalate*

- *beginnings*

- *endings*

These parts of a draft always contain cracks where a writer can insert a crowbar to open the text. On a fresh page, write one or more of these moments from scratch, lingering on physical details, emotional nuances, the environment, body language, thoughts, etc. Take your time. Then consider what portion of your new writing belongs in your project.

Before, During, After

Choose one moment in your story where a shift occurs—a change, a transformation, an epiphany. Draw a triangle in the center of a page and briefly describe that moment in the center of or below the triangle. Then draw two lines on either side, labeling one "Before" and the other "After," as shown in the illustration below.

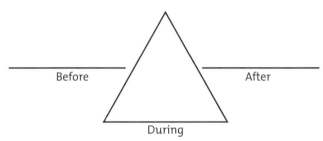

On the "Before" side, list all the bits of history and character traits that make this moment significant—the backstory. On the "After" side, list all the consequences of this moment that make it significant. What of the before and after content belongs in your project?

Conversing with a Story's Soul

So, strangely, writers must serve their stories. "No art is sunk in the self," Flannery O'Connor says, "but rather, in art the self becomes self-forgetful in order to meet the demands of the thing being seen and the thing being made." In a workshop I once attended, Mark Doty illustrated these demands by drawing an equilateral triangle on the blackboard and labeling the points "spoken," "unspoken," and "unspeakable." "These are the forces at work in any piece of literature," he said. The dynamic between these three makes stories come alive.

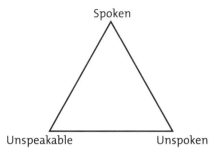

Spoken

Unspeakable   Unspoken

As I understand it, the "spoken" is the outer story—the external, conscious aspects of the narrative, the plot. The "unspoken" is subtext, or what the author wishes us to read between the lines. Subtext is developed through hints, omissions, imagery, tensions, and other features the author weaves in to enrich the story's emotional life. The author is aware of this material and intentional about crafting it.

I love that Doty also included the "unspeakable," that realm we can sense but cannot name. Mystery—what we *don't* know—permeates all creativity, but because we can't adequately define or describe it, we avoid discussing it. We associate the unspeakable with horror perhaps because we are frightened by our inability to grasp it. The territories of the spirit, of profound emotion, of the natural world, of birth and death, evil, intimacy, and human relationships—language cannot do justice to these subjects. While we can lend words to the unspeakable, even doing so with elegance and art, we ultimately fail. All writers, Doty says, attempt the impossible—to venture where there is no language.

Here also lie our shadows, our hidden truths, and, often, our brilliance.

Our collective unconscious also lurks in the unspeakable realm. Images that appear on the page, drawn from reality or the imagination, tap into archetypes beyond our awareness. Every narrative is a lens into the human story. I love how the narrator in Zora Neale Hurston's *Their Eyes Were Watching God* talks about Janie, the main character: "She didn't read books so she didn't know that she was the world and the heavens boiled down to a drop."

All this unspeakable—or, as Charles Baxter calls it, "unthinkable"—material becomes a story's gravitational center. "An unthinkable thought is not one that hasn't occurred to somebody, nor is it a thought that someone considers to be wrong. An unthinkable thought threatens a person's entire existence and is therefore subversive and consequently *can* be thought of and *has* been thought of, but has been pushed out of the mind's currency and subsumed into its margins where it festers." **Behind the words we've chosen for the page and the words we've deliberately *not* written lies a hidden tale of motivation, longing, and mystery—which we must attend in order to serve the story**.

Let's look at "An Unspoken Hunger," a piece of short creative nonfiction by Terry Tempest Williams, to get a better handle on these ideas. Please keep in mind that, unlike your work in progress, this paragraph has been polished.

It is an unspoken hunger we deflect with knives—one avocado between us, cut neatly in half, twisted then separated from the large wooden pit. With the green fleshy boats in hand, we slice vertical strips from one end to the other. Vegetable planks. We smother the avocado with salsa, hot chiles at noon in the desert. We look at each other and smile, eating avocados with sharp silver blades, risking the blood of our tongues repeatedly.

What's *spoken* here—the outer story—is obvious: Two people cut open an avocado and eat it with salsa. They're in the desert. They eat with knives. We're told outright that these people "deflect" an "unspoken hunger"—there's more to this scene than meets the eye.

A lot is *unspoken* in this piece. The intimacy of sharing an avocado, the image of a whole fruit cut in two, and sensual words like *fleshy* and *smother* imply that these people are a couple. Since they're eating with knives in the desert, we imagine them on a picnic. The couple smiles at each other, leading us to presume that they delight in the taste of the avocado and in each other. But that sentence also ends with the risk of cutting their tongues, "repeatedly," suggesting delight in the danger as well.

Underneath all this sits an unspeakable mystery. What is this hunger the couple deflects by eating avocado? Surely it's more than hunger for food. Is it carnal hunger, luscious and sharp? The avocado, with its fat, round pit, is a pregnant image; perhaps the couple is toying with some new delightful and dangerous course of action. Even if Williams is withholding information from the reader, the sweet, complex emotions of this moment are indescribable—ultimately mysterious.

What's the heartbeat of this little piece? What gives it energy and unity? I'd say it's about the simultaneous delight and danger of feeding deep hungers, although there's no single, correct answer.

Writing gets its spark when the ineffable stuff of our interior is reconciled with our material lives.

Exercise

Holy Longing

Pico Iyer once quipped, "If you have a longing, satisfaction is likely to be a disappointment." Our longings motivate and focus us. I suspect true desire is only ever inflamed, never satisfied, and that this is good. Reflect: What longing drives you to write this project? Sketch out a possible trajectory for this longing in which it is augmented rather than resolved. What might this look like? How might you broaden your longing? Why might this be helpful?

Articulating the Heartbeat

Before I begin revising, I attempt to formulate my project's heartbeat into one or two simple sentences on a bright sticky note and place it over my writing desk. This note steers me. Of every sentence, paragraph, section, and chapter I rewrite, I ask, how does this serve my heartbeat?

Of course we can't possibly know a piece's heartbeat early on. Our awareness of the heartbeat grows as we revise. We can't know a piece's inner story and its central, unifying force until the piece is done—and sometimes not even then. Regardless, the attempt to name the heartbeat is instructive. Even an inaccurate naming provides guidance. This heartbeat is a statement of purpose—a soft intention we can follow or shift.

As my central stake grows clearer, I rewrite my heartbeat statement. Here are a few iterations from my novel:

- May 2007: There's a freedom and security we Americans don't yet know or believe in that comes from suffering and having survived.

- November 2007: This book is about how Hannah's determination relates to her fear. What she most wants is a faithful rather than a fearful relationship to the world.

- June 2008: When you're unmoored from the ethical guidance of social and legal mores, what do you lean on to determine what's right? Intuition and faith.

- May 2010: What gives birth to fear that stands in the way of faith? What gives birth to faith that overcomes fear?

Note how these statements grew more precise over time. This is the fruit of deep listening—of heeding the story's will.

Some readers will wonder whether they can save time by identifying their heartbeat at a project's beginning. Remember that heartbeats are, by their nature, discovered. This discovery process will itself lend texture and depth to your prose.

Once named, the heartbeat can inform our every decision—where to begin, what to cut, what to expand, where to end, how to structure the story, and so forth. What is this story's essential work in the world? Our job as writers is to support this through every dimension of the piece.

Exercises

Listen to Your Literal Heartbeat

Pause for a moment. Place your hand on your heart. Breathe. Listen to your breath. Feel your heartbeat. Attend to the mysterious, unified workings of your body.

Then imagine placing the essence of your book near your heart. Allow your heartbeat to infuse the book's essence. The heartbeat of your book is born of your heartbeat. Hold this image for a few moments.

Then write: In what ways is your project an extension of your own life force?

Inspiration

Inspiration is both literally and figuratively the breathing in of life. As you write, pay attention to your breathing. Sit in a manner that allows you to fill your body with breath. Imagine breath entering the body of your work much as it enters your physical body.

Tips: Naming the Heartbeat

- Use working titles and headings. Titles usually need revision; the longer we work with them, the more exact they become. Can your working title point both to the outer story and to the inner story?

- On a sticky note, write a simple sentence or question articulating your project's heartbeat. What is your piece essentially about? Be sure to include both the outer and the inner stories. Post this above your writing desk and refer to it often, asking, how is my current work serving my heartbeat? Periodically revisit and revise this sentence.

- Every inquiry letter to publishers or agents must include a concise paragraph describing the submitted project. Write this paragraph to practice articulating your piece's heartbeat. You can revise it over time and use it when you're ready to publish.

Engaging Mystery

Write what you know, but write toward what you don't know. The more I've lived with Doty's triangle, the more it helps me with revision. Our task is to grow increasingly conscious of our material—to know and author it. As we rewrite, subconscious motivations become conscious; egotistical manipulations of language—our darlings—get axed; we detach ourselves from the text. We make deliberate choices about what appears on the page, what we leave unsaid, and, as best as we're able, what lurks below the surface. When revision exposes new insights, we tap the unspeakable, thus moving its contents into the unspoken and spoken realms. I find it helpful to rename the points on Doty's triangle like this:

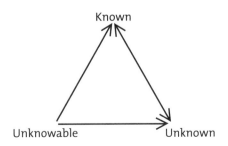

Revision harvests unknowable content, moving it to the surface and subtext. "The hidden life is, by definition, hidden," writes E. M. Forster. "The hidden life that appears in external signs is hidden no longer, has entered the realm of action. And it is the function of the novelist to reveal the hidden life at its source." In revision, we listen attentively to this hidden life and create a container for it, a story by which it can be known.

This is why we *never* know the inner story or the heartbeat in a first draft. We may sense the unknowable, but by definition it resides beyond awareness. We feel the ache but we haven't yet found the ache's story. As we pay attention to our material and read between the lines, the unknowable shines through. The unknowable is a fathomless well. The more we draw from it, the more texture and depth appear in our work, and the more aware we become of the untapped mystery remaining.[5] Just as the older we get the less we know (that is, the more we realize we don't know), the more our drafts mature the more mystery they're able to hold. Diane Glancy uses Jewish philosopher Martin Buber's terms to describe this process: "The act of revision moves a piece of writing from the I-it into the I-Thou"— that is, from an objectifying relationship into a relationship with a Sacred Other.

The slow effort of manifesting an inner story within an outer story creates art. Readers love inhabiting the spoken realm of a story, from which they can seek the unspoken and intuit the unspeakable.

---

5   Writers bat around John Keats's term "negative capability"—"when man is capable of being in uncertainties, Mysteries, doubts without any irritable reaching after fact and reason." Negative capability is essentially the ability to accept and work with the unspeakable and unknowable within our text.

They sense the author playing, creating, manipulating, and inventing. And yet the text points beyond the author, beyond even the story, to fundamental human realities.

When the writer has conversed with a great mystery, the reader slips into the seat of this mystery. Anne Frank gave her diary a name, Kitty, and imagined her to be the ideal friend with whom she could share secrets (her anger, first menstruation, dreams . . .). When I read Anne's diary, part of me imagines myself to be Anne, making beauty of a desolate world, but part of me also becomes Kitty. Anne talks to *me*; I become her friend, loyal for life.

Thus the dialogue between writer and reader happens on two planes—one conscious, the other not. I think of the writer sitting at one end of a horseshoe and the reader at the other, with the opening between them. The writer speaks directly across the gap. But there's also a subtle, underground communication that travels the length of the horseshoe, from one subconscious to another. This path is forged by the author's driving questions; it is marked by the author's tears and surprises; it is cloaked with mystery. A character in Italo Calvino's novel *If on a Winter's Night a Traveler* describes this dynamic much like Mark Doty does:

> Reading means to be ready to catch a voice that makes itself heard when you least expect it, a voice that comes from an unknown source, from somewhere beyond the book, beyond the author, beyond the convention of writing: from the unsaid, from what the world has not yet said of itself and does not yet have the words to say.

The job of literature is to give form to unnamed human experience—to say what is unsaid, or to say what has been said in a fresh and illuminating manner. The best literature uses language and gaps within language as a container to hold life's mystery.

When Annie Dillard first tried to chop wood to heat her small writing shack on an island in Puget Sound, she swung the ax and chipped ineffectively at the log. Islanders gathered to watch and laugh. Eventually, Dillard had a dream suggesting she aim not for the wood but for the chopping block. Sure enough, she could split wood that way. Her advice to writers is the same: "Aim for the chopping block. If you aim for the wood, you will have nothing. Aim past the wood, aim through the wood; aim for the chopping block." The wood is the stuff of our stories—characters, scenes, plot, subject matter, the point of view, the self. The chopping block is our common, beating heart.

Exercise

Doty's Triangle

Draw Doty's triangle on a large blank sheet of paper. Label the points "Spoken," "Unspoken," and "Unspeakable," or, if you prefer, "Known," "Unknown," and "Unknowable." Then list elements from your work in progress that you believe act as these forces. Your Unspeakable, or Unknowable, list should be made up of questions. Explore: What might you excavate from the Unspeakable or Unknowable? What is spoken or known that might be more effective as subtext? What is unspoken that might be more effective if spoken?

Toolbox: Looking for Clues

Patricia Hampl wrote this about one of her drafts:

> Now that I have the fragment down on paper, I can read this little piece as a mystery which drops clues to the riddle of my feelings, like a culprit who wishes to be apprehended. My narrative self (the culprit who invented) wishes to be discovered by my reflective self, the self who wants to understand and make sense of a half-remembered moment about a nun sneezing in the sun.

When I'm sleuthing, my conscious self searches for what my piece wants to become. What is unspoken here? What is unspeakable? What life is emerging?

Fortunately, drafts drop clues in fairly predictable places. Use this list to find "hot spots"—places that will lead you deeper into your subject. I suggest circling each of the following in your draft with a different colored pen, then answering the questions:

- *Surprises.* Where were you surprised as you were writing? Where are you surprised as you read? Why?

- *Questions.* What questions appear in the text? Why? What questions are implied? Write them out. What are you still curious to explore about this subject?

- *Powerful metaphors or images.* These are usually also

surprises—that is, not deliberately crafted. What images snag you? Why?

- *Endings.* Why did you assume your piece would end here? What if this was your beginning? How else might your piece end? What is your story's emotional conclusion? Why?

- *Beautiful prose.* We often write well when our material has energy and life. From where did these passages get their energy? Why?

- *Untold stories that carry weight.* What haven't you written that relates to your piece or sets the context? Why didn't you write it?

- *Where the story really begins.* Stories often begin long after the piece starts. Sometimes they begin before. Once you identify the real beginning, articulate for yourself *why* this is the real beginning.

- *Passages that bring up unreasonable resistance or unexpected emotion.* Strong feelings often signal significance.

These are clues to your piece's inner life. Reflect on them in your journal, dialogue with them, stretch these moments in your draft with more details—in other words, listen to what these clues say.

Exercise

Draft as Murder Mystery

Imagine that your draft is a murder mystery. You're the detective. Journal in response to these questions: What is the unsolved question you are pursuing? What clues has your draft dropped that might help you solve this mystery? Are there any pieces of evidence missing? Who are the witnesses, and what do they reveal?

CHAPTER SIX

Seeing with Others' Eyes

When my daughter was old enough to use a crayon—that is, create —I read a parenting book that analyzed adult responses to kids' achievements. Most of us look at crayon scribbles and say, "Wow! That's great!" This teaches children the delight of a final product. Sometimes we respond with, "I love it," thus emphasizing creative work's effect on an audience. The parenting expert warned us to avoid this second reaction since it can orient children's play toward pleasing others rather than themselves. She suggested instead that we respond to the child's process: "I bet making that felt good."

In my mind, all three are worthy responses. Artists need to be nurtured in their process, commended for their product, and given a sense of their impact on an audience. But when my daughter thrusts a page of scribbles in my face, the most satisfying experience for us both is when I *ooh* at the pink loop and *aah* at the brown squiggle and then say, "Tell me about this."

"It's a pencil sharpener," she says.

"And what's happening here?"

"This is the pencil, and here's Hootie sharpening it, and—Hoo! Hoo!—he flies to the owl library and . . . ."

Artists long to communicate. A pat on the back gratifies the ego but never the soul. When writers share work in progress, we want to know what we've communicated and how we might deepen the conversation.

My MFA thesis defense ranks among my most gratifying experiences as a writer. Three authors and one theologian, all of whom I held in high regard, had read my memoir. We gathered over coffee and cookies and for an hour shared an invigorating conversation about my story. What could be better? That conversation spurred two more years of revision.

Giving and Receiving Feedback

The fastest way to gain a fresh perspective on a draft is to see it through others' eyes. You'll hear contradictory advice about this, from Robert Boice's recommendation that we bounce ideas off others before even putting pen to paper to Carol Bly's tirades about writing workshops squelching inspiration. MFA programs are criticized for encouraging "writing by committee." Should we let readers in? When, and how?

I've seen far more good than harm come from writers sharing works in progress. New writers need companions; we thrive when we share struggles and victories. How else can beginners distinguish between difficulties unique to a project or to themselves, or inherent in writing? When we read others' work mid-draft, we can project ourselves into the author's seat and imagine our own solutions—an exercise that saves beginners time. Nourishing, instructive, and inspirational comments on a manuscript make a world of difference to a new writer. Feedback fuels the tank.

But soliciting readers' constructive reactions takes skill. Here are some guidelines:

1. *Don't share your work prematurely.* Seek feedback only when you can stand firmly enough in your own ideas that others' comments won't throw you off balance. Ask yourself, have I allowed enough time in that cloud of privacy and unknowing? If you're looking for someone to endorse you—to say "This work is valuable!"—don't share it. No one has the right to validate or invalidate your creativity.

2. *Your draft is good enough.* There's no point where your work *arrives* and is worthy of critique. That said, be respectful of your readers. Present a clean, spell-checked manuscript. Use standard manuscript form: twelve-point Times New Roman, double-spaced, with at least one-inch margins. Number your pages. Include your name and the date.

3. *Choose your audience carefully.* Writing is work; you need work colleagues, not cheerleaders. The best people to respond to drafts are those seriously committed to the creative process. Find peers at your level of experience or higher and teachers you respect. Note that accomplished authors often lack the skills needed to respond constructively to beginners, and that the best teachers may not have a significant body of published work.

Avoid sharing your work with family or friends. Attachment makes family members, especially parents, miserable critics. Family rarely read objectively, because love, pride, self-consciousness, and their own agendas interfere. Family tend to be more concerned about you or themselves than with the work.

Find readers who can respond to your writing as an object separate from you. My colleague Cheri Register, an excellent reader, says,

"My business as a friendly critic *is* inherently respectful: A direct, cathartic cry of sorrow calls for consolation, but a poem offered for critique deserves to be read as a poem."

The best readers open up possibilities for your text *and* for personal discovery.

If you stop writing after receiving feedback, ask yourself, "Have I stopped because I'm avoiding growing as a person or writer? Or have I stopped because I've let this reader's assessment knock down my creative process?" If you answer yes to the latter, fire your reader.

4. *Ask for stage-appropriate feedback.* Readers of a work in progress need to know your place in the work's development. Here are sample questions for the various stages:

Early drafts	What is this piece about? What might it be about? What themes do you see revealing themselves? What are you curious to have me pursue? Where do you sense untapped energy or emotion?
Mid-drafts	What is this piece about? What might it be about? How might I organize this piece around that central heartbeat? What themes have emerged? How might they be developed? What could be expanded? Why? What could be cut? Why? How might my characters be more fully realized?
Late drafts	What is this piece about? What is its heartbeat? How might my heartbeat shine through the piece's cosmetics—paragraphing, sentence structure, and word choice? How might I clean up the grammar and mechanics? Do I need an editor?

5. *Don't defend your work.* Carolyn Crane, an urban fantasy author and friend, suggests that writers receiving feedback become "learning machines, not explaining machines." Prolonged apologetics or defenses not only waste time; they also cause others to withhold their thoughts. Allow your work to stand on its own. This is why some teachers suggest that writers remain silent during the discussion of their work. While this seems unnatural to me—writers need to ask questions of their readers—I do believe writers should never mediate their work. Let your readers comment first, then ask questions.

6. *Remember that your writing has become an object separate from you.* Others' responses are addressed to your work, not to you. When a classmate asks, "When did this scene take place?" she is asking the question of the text. Write the question down. Later, consider whether or not to address the question in your writing. The work, as an independent entity, must answer for itself.

7. *Weigh your reader's biases when considering feedback.* Each of your chosen readers has strengths and biases. The poet in your writing group might make exceptional suggestions about language but not hit the mark when commenting on plot. The novelist in your group whose father just died may not give the best advice about the father-daughter conflict in your story. Know your reader. Direct your questions to tap the reader's strengths.

8. *Feedback matures with time.* When I received a professor's response to the first draft of the first chapter of my memoir, I was devastated. The pages were littered with red marks. I'd failed; my project was in shambles. Fortunately, I filed the draft away. A month later, when I dug out her comments, I was amazed. She was right! And I knew I could make the changes.

Because initial emotional reactions to comments are not always trustworthy, record or take notes while others discuss your work. Allow time to pass; reread your manuscript; respond in your journal. Then reevaluate the feedback.

9. *Develop your inner tuning fork.* The best responses to your work resonate. Always assess others' comments against your own intention or sense of the piece's heartbeat. You don't need to address every comment you're given. Use these comments to help you see the piece with fresh eyes.

Receiving feedback often goes hand-in-hand with giving feedback. While it's possible to be a fine writer without having the skills to critique others' manuscripts, gaining these skills improves your capacity to see your own work clearly. Here are a few suggestions for responding to others' work:

1. *Be a kind, intelligent, somewhat skeptical, and exceedingly curious reader.*

2. *Put yourself in the writer's shoes.* Each time you are asked for feedback, you're given a great opportunity—to experience a work in progress without having done the work. You get to imagine the pitfalls and possibilities of a project not your own, and learn from them without much sweat. Be sure to keep the writer's tastes and objectives in mind and be aware of his or her preferences. Imagining that this is your project helps you respond with grace and kindness.

3. *Be alert to the fun-house phenomenon.* Especially in group settings, an invisible judgment-warping device tends to appear in the middle of the room. Everyone else's work seems better! Remember that your voice is so familiar, it seems banal, whereas you've

never heard the interior ramblings of that young upstart next to you. New voices always dazzle. Don't be daunted. Your voice will stun that upstart.

4. *Try to articulate the heartbeat for the writer.* What is this piece essentially about for you, the reader? What might this piece become? By describing the story's core in your own language, you give the writer a tremendous gift.

5. *Ask questions that invite exploration.* As you read, pay attention to the questions that pop into your head and ask them respectfully. "Gateway questions" open up the inner story—the emotional and reflective life of characters, the emergent themes, the author's motivations. The best questions are genuine, springing from your curiosity and interest.

6. *Develop your "metareader."* Ideally, read everything twice—first for pleasure, second for craft. That is, read first as a reader, allowing yourself to be swept away by the story, and read second as a writer, identifying the choices the author made to shape your readerly response. The best feedback records both reactions.

7. *Offer specifics.* Always give examples from the text to illustrate your comments.

8. *Give success its due.* If a piece feels complete, say so. Don't nitpick.

9. *Learn from others' comments.* Seriously consider other feedback the author receives. How might it apply to your work?

A skilled reader sees beyond the printed page to the story that's emerging. Hints of what the story might become can be found in the subtext, in what's left unsaid, in powerful symbols within the draft, and even in the author's stated intention. The best readers recognize what a story is becoming and offer suggestions for manifesting that new life. The intimate discourse that began in solitude between writer and subject, between self and Mystery, continues in community.

Once you've received others' comments, I suggest these steps:

1. *Sleep on it.* The next morning, without looking at your notes, jot down and reflect on the feedback that stuck.

2. *Journal.* Consider others' comments. What resonates? What doesn't?

3. *Compile.* If you've gotten multiple readers' feedback, compile their comments into a single document. Be sure to tally overlapping comments. If you know your readers well, give each his or her own color when you copy out comments. This way, you can consider their biases as you revise.

4. *Wait.* Give the feedback breathing space.

5. *Create a revision plan.* Set goals for your next draft and create a to-do list.

6. *Begin revising.*

For all the writers who thrive in isolation, at least as many (judging from acknowledgment pages) need a village to raise a book. Without the writing group I've participated in for twenty years, I would be a poorer writer and lonelier person. I believe slow, carefully considered interaction with a respectful audience can teach us to write, develop our projects, and thrive as artists.

A Caveat for Sharing Nonfiction

When discussing personal narrative, it's far too easy for readers to comment on the author's life rather than on the written work. To help readers remember the distinction, many authors ask that the "I" of their stories be referred to as "the narrator" or "the character" rather than "you." The question "I wonder why the narrator is angry in this scene?" is gentler and more instructive than "Why are you so angry?" This formality helps the author and those critiquing focus on the crafted persona, and gain and sustain emotional distance from the story.

That said, the best feedback for creative nonfiction writers asks for serious examination of our lives rather than surface manipulation of our text. When seeking the truth of an experience, we don't want emotional distance; we want passionate engagement. For this reason, I suggest using more guarded language in conversation with others but then asking ourselves the tough personal questions later on. Why *was* I angry? Had I been aware of my anger? Did my anger have consequences?

If readers veer into judgments about your life or suggest that you alter facts, take charge. Call attention to what is happening. Ask them to return to the text. If a group is unable to stay focused on the text, they're apt to do more damage than good.

Hearing with Others' Ears

When a writer entrusts me with a manuscript, I read it, write comments in the margin, take notes, and compile my thoughts in a letter. Then, when we meet, I begin by asking: What's happened with this project since you gave it to me? Any new insights? Any new questions? Whether because of my open-ended invitation or the inevitable time lag, writers usually disclose helpful information. A twenty-to-thirty-minute conversation about how a project is evolving (what it's about, why they're writing it, what's on the page and what isn't, what they're learning as they write) is often more instructive about next steps than going over my written feedback.

"Talk it" is how Meredith Sue Willis describes this process. Many authors are leery of discussing their work, and rightly so—it's possible to foreclose on your discoveries by relating a story aloud before it's written. Remember to honor the cloud of privacy and unknowing. However, most projects reach a point when discussion is a useful tool. The story is on the page. Talking is a different medium, and a new medium brings new perspective.

Once again, choose your listener carefully. The most productive conversations come when the listener responds not to the work or the writer but rather to the relationship between work and writer. You want a listener who is able to hear beyond the surface story for what is unknowable—for what has not yet been written. The quality of listening another person brings to your work affects the quality of your insights as you discuss it.

Exercises

The Elevator Speech

Find a trustworthy listener. In one minute, tell that person what your piece is about, both its outer and inner stories. Afterward, take notes on what you said. Any new insights? Can you condense your description even further?

The Imaginary Therapist

Between drafts of your work, imagine telling a therapist or spiritual director what you're working on. Write the conversation out. What does your counselor ask about your project? How do you respond?

Extended Metaphors

If a metaphor plays an important role in your story, try this: Without going into any detail, name the metaphor to two or more friends and ask them to free-associate in response. Write down their ideas, then journal in response. Do others' thoughts about this image give you any new ideas?

Toolbox: Creating a Revision Guide and Style Sheet

Our brains can hold only so much information. Thank the stars for paper and pen!

Revision Guide

I recommend the revision guide as a tool for collecting thoughts and steering revision. The revision guide is a strategic plan. It holds our vision for the next draft and lists the concrete tasks that will implement this vision. The guide orients rather than dictates. Setting an intention can go a long way in shaping an outcome.

Here are suggestions for what your revision guide might contain:

1. *A simple sentence articulating the heartbeat.* Or a simple image representing the book's essence.

2. *Important themes and questions.* You can list or illustrate these and refer to them throughout your revision process. Do you stay faithful to your themes and questions from beginning to end?

   For example, here are some revision notes I made between the second and third drafts of *Hannah, Delivered*.
   - Hannah: "I didn't want faith, I wanted certainty, to know I was making the right decision."
   - Where there's fear, underneath is the desire to control something.

   In the revision that followed, I wanted to make sure Hannah behaved according to her desire for certainty. I wanted to figure out how Hannah's fear led her to attempts to control her circumstances. My revision guide helped me stay on track.

3. *Movement in ideas and characters.* Where do the ideas you're exploring begin? How do they evolve? Where do they land? Who are the characters in your story? How do they change? Where do they arrive? What are your emotional relationships to each of these ideas or characters at the beginning, middle, and end of your piece? Again, examples from *Hannah, Delivered:*
   - H works from a right-wrong, good-bad, polarized way of thinking about the world (judging parents,

others, self)➔she discovers realm of faith, which takes her beyond legalistic thinking.

- H immobilized by fear➔H mobilized by will but governed by fear➔H creates false fear structure to give self freedom➔H acts from love

You may choose to show movement in ideas and characters visually, with a map, flowchart, or collage.

4. *Guidance.* If there's any material (from your journal, from your reading) that informs your thinking about this project, include it here. This allows you to be inspired by material without having to quote it in the text.

5. *Lists of large changes.* These can be concrete tasks for specific scenes:
   - Create a clear picture of Hannah right away.
   - Have Hannah imagine scenarios about her birth earlier, to explain her lack of surprise when she learns the truth.

   Or they can be tasks for the entire book:
   - Who does Hannah know in town? Friends? Round out the social dimension of her character.
   - Show Hannah needing affirmation from the midwives throughout. Keep her character consistent.

   Small changes to the text are better kept as marginal notes on a single hard copy.

6. *Lists of tics.* We all have writing tics that appear regularly in our work as well as tics particular to a project.

These may be images, character gestures, word choices, sentence structures, etc., that we repeat unconsciously. Keep a running list of your tics to address later in the revision process. Here are a few images and words I tend to overuse:

- straining chair-back springs
- emotional swings at chapter endings
- face flaring with heat
- shrug
- dread
- flutter

7. *Scraps, notes to self, ideas, and reminders.* The revision guide is the place to gather this miscellany. If you cross off items as you address them rather than deleting them, you can view them for later reconsideration.

The order of this list is intentional. Prioritize large tasks that will radically change the manuscript and hold back on polishing scenes and language. Do triage. Don't spend days perfecting a scene you'll later slice.

I like to print out the revision guide and keep it on my desk (that is, in my face) while I rewrite. But I also keep an open, active copy on the computer so I can add tics, dump rejected passages, and make notes on the fly. Create a system that is responsive to your working style.

Style Sheet

In addition to creating a revision guide, which is project specific, I recommend that you keep an ongoing record of stylistic tics and shortcomings. Rather than wasting brain space worrying whether you're using *which* and *that* correctly, make a note about the issue on your style sheet. When you reach the editing stage, use your style sheet as a proofing checklist. You can use the word processor's "find" function to ferret out these mistakes.

Here are a few of mine, with advice borrowed from Strunk and White's *The Elements of Style*:

- Eliminate *the fact that*.

- Eliminate *who is, who was, which is, which was*.

- Too frequent use of *but* as a conjunction. Search ", but".

- Don't use *like* as a conjunction. *Like* governs nouns and pronouns. Before phrases and clauses the equivalent word is *as*. *As if* often works, too.

- *Which*—nondefining, nonrestrictive. *That*—defines, restricts.

- Search *is, was, were*—"to be" verbs. Can I use more lively language?

Early Revisions and the Big Changes

CHAPTER SEVEN

Reframing

In a 2009 TED Talk, the Nigerian novelist Chimamanda Ngozi Adichie considers the human inclination to tell a "single story" about others, especially those we barely know. When she arrived in the United States for college, her roommate was surprised by her ability to use a stove and to speak English well. "Her default position toward me, as an African, was a kind of patronizing, well-meaning pity." The roommate's single story of Africa was one of tragedy and poverty. Single stories are the stuff of stereotypes, "and the problem with stereotypes is not that they are untrue, but that they are incomplete. They make one story become the only story."

The same fallacy occurs in writing. A first draft is a single story. Revision insists that we reject the single story in favor of layered, complex, and contradictory stories. Just as intimacy and awareness break down stereotypes, intimacy with and awareness of our material break apart our oversimplifications and half-truths. The central work of early revision is to discover radically new ways to see—and respect—the subject.

In college, my fellow English majors and I were required to write a forty-page analytical paper for our senior comprehensive exam. None of us had written anything that long before, so a professor gave us a pep talk. Up until that point I'd avoided him; he had a reputation for hole-punching misused words out of student essays or cutting poor papers into confetti and returning them in sealed plastic baggies. At this lecture, he suggested that we state the paper's thesis in an introductory paragraph. For forty pages we were to write the body of the essay, comparing various works of literature. We were to conclude with a summary of our findings.

"Then," he said, "take a pair of scissors and cut off the final paragraph. Paste it to a fresh sheet of paper and start over."

We moaned.

Twenty-some years later I've come to appreciate his advice. "The time to begin writing an article," according to Mark Twain, "is when you have finished it to your satisfaction. By that time you begin to clearly and logically perceive what it is you really want to say." We frequently arrive at worthy ideas at the end of a draft—that nice twist at the conclusion, the bit of inner story that finally rears its head. Therapists tell me that the last five minutes of a session are the most revealing. The patient turns on his way out the door and blurts, "I'm really jealous of my brother . . ." Drafts work this way too. Whenever I give in-class exercises, I alert students two minutes before the time's up. They tell me that's when their best insights arrive.

The trouble is, we like the *aha* landing. We're reluctant to mess with it. But that scary English professor knew fully developed layers of insight are more gratifying than a single, final hoorah. He knew that any thesis (or heartbeat) we might posit will be fundamentally changed by forty pages of research and thought. If we take the insights of a first draft as the premise of our second draft, we will arrive at other aha's. Multiple insights mean multiple dimensions of meaning.

This is the work of reframing. We look through a new lens and our material shifts. Each revision finds a new lens to better serve the story.

A student of mine once shared what was to become the opening chapter of her memoir, in which she described a family reunion. Our class read about dozens of relatives, endured pages of happy conversation, and only in the last paragraph learned that, within a year of this party, three of these relatives died and two more were hospitalized because of chemical overdoses. The author was writing to learn why.

The class agreed that the final paragraph was her emotional hook; without it, we simply didn't care about the reunion. What if she moved her bombshell of information up front?

She agreed to try. The following week she reported how this new placement changed the scene. With the stake disclosed up front, whole pages of glib dialogue became unnecessary. She homed in on those details that furthered her exploration—who was drinking how much, the jealousy and hurt roiling beneath cheery conversations, the untold histories of addiction. Reframing brought her closer to the scene's truth.

A few weeks later she burst into class. "My story doesn't start with the reunion at all!" she announced. "It starts after the funeral of one of my relatives, when a cousin and I were sitting on the church steps. I wondered aloud who would be next. Then I asked myself, 'Why? Why is this happening to my family?' *That's* the start of my story."

This writer found her beginning not at the chronological launch of events but at the origin of her quest. This reframed her memoir yet again; it shifted the structure, the narrative voice, and the story's emotional engine. She knew the idea would work because it placed her quest—her impetus for writing—front and center.

The work of listening deeply to a draft alters our focus. To say this another way, awareness of the inner story changes how we see the outer story and affects how it must be told. We then generate new, increasingly relevant text and eliminate text that has become extraneous. Reframing shifts the center of gravity, highlighting the details that bear weight, adding connective tissue, reflecting on the story as a whole rather than in parts, and otherwise working to serve the heartbeat.

Sometimes an early draft avoids central and essential material. I once had a student who wrote a delightful piece about her family car. Her father had been an auto mechanic who cared for his Dodge so well the odometer had turned over three times in thirty years. This was the only car the author had known during childhood. Her small group was in stitches over her anecdotes. But then someone asked, "Why are you writing this?" She burst into tears; a week earlier she had taken the Dodge to the junkyard. The group was floored. This information gave her story drive, emotional resonance, and present-day relevance. These weren't sentimental memories; they were part of a grieving process that looked through the old car to a family togetherness the author had lost. By omitting *why* she was writing, she'd avoided the piece's central stake. Her loss reframed her material. It demanded to be written.

Usually the orientation of individual parts of a manuscript shifts once those pieces are positioned together. I originally wrote the chapter of my memoir about biking across Wales thinking my whole book would be about biking. My early draft emphasized externals like the strain on my body, the people I met, and my growing sense of independence. Only later did I figure out that my book was really about how my sexual identity informed my faith. I had to view my biking stories through this lens, eliminating anecdotes that didn't serve this purpose and polishing those that did until they illustrated how my physical and spiritual being came alive over those months of solitude. Although I was working with a fairly well-developed draft, it looked as though I was writing from scratch.

At times extreme craft changes help writers reframe their stories. An editor at Riverhead Books received a memoir written by an Afghani doctor named Khaled Hosseini. The story was good but she recognized that it could be great if it didn't adhere to the facts. She shared her ideas with Hosseini; he ran with them and wrote *The Kite Runner.*

When E. B. White initially wrote *Charlotte's Web*, he had a tough time beginning the novel. In one version it started with Charlotte; in another, with Wilber; in a third, with a rhapsody about life in the barn; in a fourth, with the farmer walking to the hoghouse to count a new litter of pigs. Only after many false starts did White latch on to Fern Arable, the eight-year-old who begs her father to spare the runt of a new litter of pigs, and pen what Lauren Winner calls one of the best opening lines in American fiction: "Where's Papa going with that ax?" White unlocked the novel by reframing his material.

The history of fiction is loaded with tales of radical reframing: a minor character becoming the main character, the point of view shifting from omniscient to first person, the addition or subtraction of time in the narrator's vantage on the story, tense changing from past to present, and the like. Such manipulation of craft elements succeeds only when it serves the story's heartbeat. Harper

Lee's *To Kill a Mockingbird* is a fine example. Her first draft, recently published as *Go Set a Watchman*, was set twenty years later. Scout is a disillusioned adult, Atticus spews racial bigotry, Jem is dead, and the central events of *Mockingbird* are passing asides in *Watchman*. This early version was so radically reframed that we can now read it as a separate novel. Revision took Lee's draft from a bitter, ax-grinding tale into a morally complex coming-of-age story with tremendous staying power.

"Revision is like putting up a house, then realizing that the walls aren't plumb and the windows don't hang right," writes David Michael Kaplan.

> What to do? Tear it all apart, start over? Who wants to? *But you must*, the good writing angel perched on your shoulder whispers. *Just leave it*, coaxes the bad writing angel on your other shoulder. *Maybe the owners won't notice.* Except you, my friend, are the owner. You have to live there. And maybe you can. But don't expect anyone else to.

If we want our stories to be habitable and hospitable, if we want the life they contain to thrive, we almost always must reframe the house.

Exercises

Reorienting Ourselves and the Map of Experience

When my partner had cancer, she participated in an art therapy group that asked her to paint her illness. Emily's image showed blocked light being overshadowed by darkness. She hated it. Then the instructor turned her painting upside down. Suddenly it looked "like a bright blessing washing up on a fertile shore."

The exercise gave her permission to see her image from a new vantage and to continue shaping it. Later she wrote, "At last I feel like a true artist. I no longer am at the mercy of images around and within me. I am now shaping them, holding them in a bigger story, a bigger love."

When in your life have you known this kind of radical reframing? Have you ever experienced this in your writing or other art-making? Explore these stories.

The Reframing Experiment

In your current draft, identify one of the following:

- *an insight that arrives in the final pages*

- *an important element—information, an emotion—that is part of your story but not present in the draft*

- *an image that evokes your story's central theme or exploration*

- *an event that occurs well into your story that illustrates the central conflict*

- *a line of dialogue, description, or reflection that speaks not just to the scene but also to the project as a whole*

In the spirit of experimentation, rewrite beginning with this element. Even if this experiment fails, pay attention to new material that arises. How does this frame help you see your content in a fresh way?

Blind Rewrite

Without looking at your manuscript, consider an important passage —a climax, a beginning, an ending, a significant moment. Write this passage again from scratch—again, without looking at your draft. Don't try to re-create what you've already written. Instead, write it from a new angle; pay closer attention to sensory details or internal thoughts and feelings or to the moment's significance. Don't worry if the new draft seems worse than the first. The point of this exercise is not to improve your text but rather to generate new insights.

The Genre Experiment

Take your piece and recast it in a new genre. Try one or more of the following:

- *a screenplay*
- *a personal essay*
- *a poem*
- *a letter to a friend*
- *a novel or short story*
- *a list*
- *a feature article for a newspaper*
- *a graphic novel*

Even if your recast piece fails, the new genre may give you fresh material or a new approach to old material. For instance, rewriting a scene as a screenplay forces you to focus on dramatic dialogue, and rewriting prose into poetry forces concision and attention to language and imagery.

Toolbox: Writing While Overwhelmed

At some point most prose writers feel overwhelmed. Except for those deliberately writing short, stand-alone pieces, writers face projects whose scope or subject matter is larger than most humans can fathom. The memories are too complex, the emotions too fearsome, the pages too many, the plots too elaborate, the themes too interconnected, the motivations too secret. The inadequacy of our drafts coupled with the mind's inability to encompass complex, book-length thoughts for extended periods causes many writers to shut down. The work is simply too hard.

When writers hire me hoping I'll fix this, I tell them three things. First, **don't we *want* our work to be bigger than us?** The best writing addresses universal truths; it digs down to the foundation of our humanity; it asks questions that have been with us since the beginning of time. Literature always connects the personal to the universal, the telling detail to the broadest abstraction. The fact that we're overwhelmed means we're doing good work, or at least work that matters.

Second, **every project, no matter how overwhelming, has entry points that are manageable**. I've yet to encounter a subject that can't be broken down into smaller pieces—taken "bird by bird," as Anne Lamott's father advised when her brother was daunted by a grade-school assignment. Here are a few mechanical suggestions:

- Rather than striving to create complete chapters, begin with small chunks of text. Ken Atchity calls these "islands." I prefer Scott Russell Sanders's coarser term, "chunks," because it sounds even less complete. Moments, scenes, character descriptions, and exposition can exist as independent entities in a draft. You can always build transitions and connections later if you need to. Label your chunks so you can find them.

- Consider using a drafting application like Scrivener, which allows you to easily draft, see, and move chunks of text. Or configure your files in a word processing program to better serve a large project:

  - If you've drafted parts of your manuscript in separate computer files, copy and paste all your material into a single file.

  - Give chunks of text headings. Most word processing programs now have a navigation tool that works like a menu on the web, making it easy to move through large manuscripts and automatically generate a table of contents.

  With all your material in one place, you can search and find text, move chunks around, and see your work in its entirety.

- If you are writing by hand, create an outline or catalogue. Use a binder with tabs or an accordion file with labels.

- If you're typing on a computer, periodically print your document with page numbers and a table of contents. Use labeled sticky notes or folder tabs to organize the hard copy.

As writers we have to physically manage large quantities of text. Here are a few other practical suggestions:

- Once you've compiled readers' feedback on a single manuscript, discard all other copies.

- Once you've made the changes from a hard copy onto the computer—and backed your computer up off site— discard or file the draft.

- Only save landmark hard copy drafts. Date them.

Third, change your process. Every piece has an anatomy, an intricate amalgam of organs and muscles and nerves, and the interconnected workings of this anatomy become evident only once a significant portion is written. In our first draft, we compose a liver and toenail and the sense of smell; we create a limb, a chapter that functions well on its own but is disembodied. At some point (different for each writer and each book), we grow aware of the need for connective tissue—to hook up these body parts and get them communicating. We intuit the whole but know the pages before us do not yet represent this whole.

The writing process that initially served us well rarely works as our projects develop. Revision entails shifting *how* we write, not just *what* we write.

When the old tools no longer work, many writers assume they're stuck. But the work at each stage is significantly different, demanding new tools and new methods. In my case, I often turn back to pen and paper to generate changes; I can no longer write in snatches of time but need two- or three-hour blocks; I trace narrative arcs or thematic movements, adding and deleting text across diverse sections of a manuscript; I need to work with images (maps, outlines, sketches) rather than words; I scan the manuscript to trace each character's inner life. Remember when you discovered and came to peace with your own unique process of generating? Now you need to discover and come to peace with your unique revision process.

Spend an hour brainstorming *how* you write in your notebook. What are your current needs? What approach might best suit those needs?

In early revisions I suggest reentering your material whimsically, randomly, guided more by instinct and desire than by order. What passages move you to probe further? Which feed your curiosity?

In later revisions you will be well served by progressing from beginning to end, building transitions between chunks of text, and tracing the development of themes or emotions or tension.

The key to moving forward on a project is accepting the overwhelming feeling while at the same time finding small, practical portals into the work. Remember, **we**

don't want to rid ourselves of Mystery; we want to enter it, look around, and offer our readers small glimpses. Successful writers experience discomfort and proceed regardless.

CHAPTER EIGHT

Practicing Presence

Revision asks that we show up more fully on the page.

Everyone balks when I say this. Memoirists do their best to downplay the self as main character; writing about the self is, well, *selfish*; why would a reader want more? Fiction writers are in the business of imagining new people in new circumstances; the author, they assume, has no place in their stories. We're taught not to call attention to ourselves—doing so is inconsiderate or sinful and certainly not the stuff of art. Most writers assume the elements of good literature reside outside themselves, in craft or content, and so imagine revision as maneuvering text in response to readers' needs.

But every story worth its salt looks through a self onto our shared reality. We need a fully present self to create a transparent and accurate view.

"The more you wish to describe a Universal the more minutely and truthfully you must describe a Particular," Brenda Ueland asserts. We humans are embodied creatures. To enter a story, readers need eyes to see with and feet to walk around on. The primary particular of any story is its main character—in creative nonfiction, the I representing the author; in fiction, a character constructed, consciously or otherwise, from traits and ruminations and observations of the author. Characters have feet planted in muddy mud; they live out the more abstract realms of emotions, ideas, and relationships within bodily, sensory existence. In storytelling, the personal doesn't sit at one end of a seesaw across from the universal; the personal embodies the universal. Human experience encompasses truth. We pass through mud and grit and bones—the lens of humanity—to give a story life.

In revision writers sharpen our human lens by inhabiting the essence and origins of our characters. Underneath craft and content choices lies our bare relationship to the material. Showing up on the page is the literary version of being fully present—of attending so completely to the people and circumstances of the story that we forget ourselves entirely. You have to be present to evoke Presence.

Showing Up

As simple as it sounds, **showing up—bringing a full heart and open mind to one's immediate circumstances, heeding one's feelings, being *real*, in real time—is exceedingly difficult**. We are governed by fear and hang-ups and misunderstandings. Usually we do our best to avoid what's happening here and now.

This avoidance is always evident in early drafts. A rough draft is like a blind date; we're cautious about sharing intimate secrets and touch—rightly so. In revision, we deepen the relationship by listening to our material and by bringing ourselves forward. In creative nonfiction we show up literally; in fiction, figuratively.

Let's first trace this path in memoir. For years I worked with a student who helped people with mental disabilities form and live in a cooperative community; she wrote as part of her job, to create a record of how these individuals were changed by communal living. Reading these stories to community members gave her great satisfaction. In class I tried to persuade her to include her own experience; who was this person buying up houses and supporting these quirky people to live independently, often for the first time? What had inspired her to do this for more than thirty years? She resisted. Readers wouldn't care about her. Besides, she wanted to honor these remarkable people who were so often dismissed. "I don't have time to be selfish or impractical," she said.

Almost all beginning memoirists face similar resistance. They want to focus on a family member or friend; they want to relate some dramatic event or extraordinary idea, and so they downplay their own role in the story. They bypass the self out of embarrassment, humility, disinterest, or concern for the reader. Memoirs, they complain, have too many I's.

During our last week of class, this woman tried an experiment. She wrote about how her prejudices were overturned when the community welcomed an autistic man. With the addition of herself as a character, her writing acquired new energy. All her characters became more real. The class was so moved, they stood and clapped.

Why?

First, she eliminated the pretense of omniscience. In her earlier stories, she had avoided the I because she wanted her mentally disabled housemates to take center stage. She asked her readers, who know a human composed the stories, to suspend their curiosity about the author's relationship to the subject.

The contemporary reader has grown intolerant of the suspension of belief that this detached point of view requires. The erasure of the I is a distortion, a falsification even. Henry David Thoreau writes in his introduction to *Walden*, "In most books the *I*, or first person, is omitted; in this it will be retained. . . . We commonly do not remember that it is, after all, always the first person that is speaking." Feminism's gift to academia is its insistence on naming the cultural lens of any study; the personal experience of the scholar always shapes the results. Even scientists wrestle with this phenomenon: A nuclear physicist observing the movement of subatomic particles affects their direction; an anthropologist observing cultural events influences what happens. **We now understand truth in relationship rather than isolation**.

How much more so when our subject is our own experience! "I favor the first person," writes Graham Swift about his novels. "One reason I do so is that I do not want simply to tell, out of the blue, a story. I want to show the pressure and need for its telling—I am as interested in the narrator as in the narrative. I want to explore the urgency of the relation between the two." Contrary to what we expect, the essence of drama is not located in the events of your life or your character's life but in the way the story is told. Likewise, aesthetic pleasure is revealed and created in relationship. The painter Robert Henri cautions students not to "try to paint *good landscapes*. Try to paint canvases that will show how interesting landscape looks to you—your pleasure in the thing." The life force of literature is the urgent dynamic between writer and subject. Why does the writer care? That's why the reader will care.

By becoming a player in her own story, my student offered up her shoes (her affection for her housemates, her prejudices, her humble change of heart) for the reader to walk in. Note how unselfish—how generous, in fact—this really is. The I isn't the story's focus. It's our best means of focusing.

For years I reviewed stacks of applications to a two-year apprenticeship in creative nonfiction. Usually the stories were told plainly: This happened, then this, then this. My husband had a heart attack. My child was diagnosed with attention deficit disorder. I lost my job. "And?" I wanted to ask. Events form a record, not a story. I want to know what the writer *makes* of these events. I want to know the story the *writer* makes, not just the story life has made. I want to see (or at least sense) the wizard behind the curtain offering himself as a vulnerable, mistaken, wise, and blundering companion.

When we revise creative nonfiction, we must bring ourselves forward. We must render our subject well, and we must develop the relationship between self and subject.

In the example above, note how my student's sense of audience shifted from specific people to no one, the self, anyone, everyone. She no longer wrote for some practical purpose (to record her community's history) but rather as part of a personal quest. By surrounding herself with a cloud of privacy, she could appear in her story with integrity. **The act of listening to our innermost questions, of tracing memory or emotion or imagination, of creating for the sake of creation helps us make stories that are honest, complex, and captivating**.

In fiction this work is more fanciful and subterranean. Fiction writers create and flesh out their characters using their imaginations, but the origin of their characters' life force is the same as in nonfiction: the author's psyche.

Many people assume that good plot makes a good story. Throw in action, tension, and mystery and you've got it made. But thrilling events (murders, adventures, trysts) can be rendered impotent by a shallow character or a narrator without personality or an author's unappealing worldview. Other people insist that a unique voice makes a good story, and like a fast-paced plot, an innovative voice has great allure. Who doesn't love a new sound, a fresh style, an unconventional lens? But plot and voice and all other craft elements are effective only when they reveal the passion and tension in characters' responses to events.

What is the source of this passion and tension? The author's life. Every created character can be traced back to some dimension of the author's being. "The characters in my novels are my own unrealized possibilities," Milan Kundera writes in *The Unbearable Lightness of Being*. "That is why I am equally fond of them all and equally horrified by them. Each one has crossed a border that I myself have circumvented."

Revision asks that we allow our characters to fully reveal themselves. We do this by entering completely into their bodies, histories, personalities, and worldviews. What about this character hooks your heart? What is this story's emotional origin? Knowing *your* part in the subject helps you understand your character's part. Knowing *your* borders, and which your character has crossed, heightens your stake. Without this awareness, writers remain disengaged, and disengagement is always evident to a reader.

While fiction writers' lives, personalities, and decisions might be radically different from that of their characters, nevertheless fiction writers must *care*. Our investment in our characters' circumstances can't be manufactured; it must be real. The passionate self must show up. Here's Ray Bradbury's explanation:

When honest love speaks, when true admiration begins, when excitement rises, when hate curls like smoke, you need never doubt that creativity will stay with you for a lifetime. The core of your creativity should be the same as the core of your story and of the main character in your story. What does your character want, what is his dream, what shape has it, and how expressed? Given expression, this is the dynamo of his life, and your life, then, as Creator. At the exact moment when truth erupts, the subconscious changes from wastebasket file to angel writing in a book of gold.

Consider how *Anna Karenina* conveys a multifaceted portrait of Tolstoy's inner life, or how thoroughly we inhabit Jane Austen's morality and social awareness when reading her novels. Or Charles Dickens's relationship to David Copperfield:

Whether I shall turn out to be the hero of my own life, or whether that station will be held by anybody else, these pages must show. To begin my life with the beginning of my life, I record that I was born (as I have been informed and believe) on a Friday, at twelve o'clock at night. It was remarked that the clock began to strike, and I began to cry, simultaneously.

Readers immediately enter Copperfield's persona, which we sense both is and isn't Dickens's, and our own. Right away I wonder, "Am I the hero of my own life? How can I know?" I keep reading to find out. Dickens wouldn't have Copperfield ask this question if he himself weren't interested, nor would he if he didn't find Copperfield a useful means for examining the world. Dickens, in all his curiosity and whimsy and social criticism, participates in his stories.

Point of view is a choice. Showing up isn't.

No matter how authors cloak themselves, by downplaying the I or using a royal we or creating fictional characters, the self is a central player in the making of literature. Really, it's all we have.

Exercises

Showing Up in Creative Nonfiction and First Person Fiction

Scan your manuscript for places writers commonly don't show up:

- The "we" of childhood and crowds. *Are there moments in your story where you lose your main character in a group? The I often dissolves into we when we write about siblings or friends from childhood. Even when you are certain the group shared a feeling or a thought, remember that your reader can experience the group through only one individual. Remain faithful to your character's perspective while also describing what happens for the group.*

- The pompous "we." *Do you make grandiose statements using first person plural? Consider them carefully. Will every reader feel included in the we? Might your pronouncements carry more authority if written in first person singular? Authors* should *make bold declarations about the human condition—with deliberation.*

- The omniscient narrator. *Where do you attempt a nonjudgmental, distanced, personalityless voice? Beginning memoirists and essayists sometimes try to look at their material from outside themselves. Don't. Your self—your voice—is what gives your work pizzazz.*

- The narrator. *Some beginning writers get so caught up in writing* what happened, *they forget to reflect on why the story is important. If you're writing creative nonfiction or fiction in the first person, consider developing the narrator as a persona. Who is telling your story, and why?*

- The character. *Some beginning writers, especially avid journal keepers, never leave the narrator's perspective. Remember that your reader needs a character's body to inhabit the story. Whether you are writing about a younger self, a present-day self, or a fictional character, be sure to create that person for your reader and place the character in scenes.*

Showing Up in Our Characters

Every image that appears in our dreams represents some facet of the self. Likewise with characters. In your notebook reflect on each of your characters: What might this character have to teach you? What does this character want from your story, or from you?

To take the Jungian analysis one step further, the characters that appear in our dreams (and fiction) usually contain archetypes—prototypes of human personality or behavior present since the beginning of time. Readers recognize themselves in archetypal qualities within fictional characters; this is one way the particulars of a fictional story tap into universal truths. Investigate how your characters manifest certain archetypes:

- *Where does the hero appear? Why?*

- *Where does the trickster appear? Why?*

- *The devil?*

- *The wise one?*

- *The great mother?*

- *The child?*

- *Who is the primary self your reader inhabits?*

- *Where does the self's shadow side appear—qualities the self does not identify with but nonetheless possesses?*

Relating to Characters

Newbery Medal–winner Kate DiCamillo believes that "the writer must love her characters, must open her heart to them, give the whole of herself to them, in order for those characters to give themselves back to her." Take time to explore your relationship to your characters. Why do you love them? What about them do you dislike, and why? In what way are you similar and different? Who in your life does each character most remind you of? Why? What might you have to learn from each character?

Quick Versions

If you're writing creative nonfiction, write two quick versions (no longer than a page, regardless of your project's length) of your story: What is the story life has given you? And what is the story you want to make of this material? Reflect on the difference.

If you're writing fiction, write two or more quick versions (no longer than a page, regardless of your project's length) of your story: If you had your way, how would this story unfold? If your main characters had their way, what would happen? What would happen if a minor character, or the setting, or some political or social force determined the story's direction? Given all the possibilities for your book's plot, which will you choose? Why?

Author, Character, Narrator

Let's return to that worn bit of writing class wisdom, "Write what you know." Don't use *material* you know; use the *passion* you know. "The memoirist, like the poet and the novelist," writes Vivian Gornick, "must engage with the world, because engagement makes experience, experience makes wisdom, and finally it's the wisdom— or rather the movement toward it—that counts." What gives a story juice? Emotional engagement.

Chances are good your initial drafts contain sparks of emotional engagement. In revision, manifest this commitment in every dimension of the work. The more you show up, the higher the stakes. You can show up within your characters, within the narrator, and as an author, a real human being.

In our day-to-day lives, we transition between many selves— from parent to neighbor to friend to coworker—without effort or awareness. Likewise in creative writing; each persona, including the I, has many facets, and we transition between them naturally. Awareness of these personas helps us make intentional choices about how and when to use them effectively.

Authors are the consciousness behind the story. You cannot shape or escape your author self. The choices you make as an author—what scenes or characters to include, when to show and when to tell, what material to make overt and what to make subtext—all reveal the wizard behind the curtain. The created text is covered with the creator's fingerprints. "We read anything looking for a pattern of events, and through it a meaning," writes Joan Silber. "Plot is how a writer indicates the ways she or he thinks the world works." Our flesh-and-bones self is a presence within our creation.

Characters are the players within a story. In fiction, characters are formed of an alchemy between real people and the author's imagination; in nonfiction, characters are creations that represent real people. Since all characters have some origin in reality, let's first look closely at memoir, where the writer becomes the main character.

Beginners find this idea absurd. "I'm *me*," they say, "not a character." But "no one is skilled enough to capture him- or herself completely on the page in all of his multi-faceted and sometimes duplicitous glory," Robin Hemley says. "The persona on the page is a representation." Because the I we find so familiar conveys nothing about our personhood to a reader, we need to introduce this person through our thoughts, actions, physical appearance, and words. To bring the two-dimensional I to life, we must create a character.

The character self is easiest to recognize in childhood memoirs. The younger self has a vantage on the world quite distinct from the writer:

> Our teacher went around the room and wrote the required letter into each one of our notebooks. When she came around to me, she printed a large A in the upper left corner of the first page of my notebook, and handed me the crayon.
>
> "I can't," I said, knowing full well that what you do with black crayons is scribble on the wall and get your backass beaten, or color around the edges of pictures, but not write.

To write, you needed a pencil. "I can't!" I said, terrified, and started to cry.

Audre Lorde depicts a four-year-old with her own particular assumptions about crayons and pencils. In the early pages of *Zami*, the girl Audre is the primary actor in events that move the story forward. She is the main character.

Likewise in your memoir; the younger self (be it years or days younger) is a player who deserves a spot center-stage without the interference or interpretation of other, older selves. At crucial moments in the story, you can focus your narrative lens closely on this character; you can allow the character to *show* what you might otherwise *tell*. Take this example from Scott Russell Sanders's essay "Under the Influence," about the store where his father bought alcohol:

> Because the Mom and Pop who ran the dump were neighbors of ours, living just down the tar-blistered road, I hated them all the more for poisoning my father. I wanted to sneak in their store and smash the bottles and set fire to the place. I also hated the Gallo brothers, Ernest and Julio, whose jovial faces shone from the labels of their wine, labels I would find, torn and curled, when I burned the trash. I noted the Gallo brothers' address, in California, and I studied the road atlas to see how far that was from Ohio, because I meant to go out there and tell Ernest and Julio what they were doing to my father, and then, if they showed no mercy, I would kill them.

Note how the character acts, thinks, and feels. Sanders says of writing childhood memories, "Don't condescend to your younger self. Your feelings back then have authority." Our character selves deserve their own opinions, foibles, feelings, and interpretation of events. They don't need us to prop them up; they can stand on their own feet. In revision, we create a well-rounded, complex portrait of the character self.

As the self we're writing about grows older, distinguishing between the character self and the narrator self becomes more difficult. Even so, that (relatively) younger self *is* distinct and needs to be portrayed as such. Here's an example from Terry Tempest Williams's *Refuge*:

> Over dessert, I shared a recurring dream of mine. I told my father that for years, as long as I could remember, I saw this flash of light in the night in the desert—that this image had so permeated my being that I could not venture south without seeing it again, on the horizon, illuminating buttes and mesas.
>
> "You did see it," he said.
>
> "Saw what?"
>
> "The bomb. The cloud. We were driving home from Riverside, California. . . ."
>
> I stared at my father.
>
> "I thought you knew that," he said. "It was a common occurrence in the fifties."
>
> It was at this moment that I realized the deceit I had been living under. Children growing up in the American Southwest, drinking contaminated milk from contaminated cows, even from the contaminated breasts of their mothers, my mother—members, years later, of the Clan of One-Breasted Women.

Note how Williams places us within an adult version of herself who is nonetheless distinct from the person writing the story. At times it's hard to tell; we're not sure whether her final sentence is the reflection of her character self in the moment or her narrator self reflecting back. But contrast this passage with another a few pages later, after Williams describes the deaths of all the women in her family. Here she speaks solidly from her narrator voice: "What I do know, however, is that as a Mormon woman of the fifth generation of Latter-day Saints, I must question everything, even if it means losing my faith, even if it means becoming a member of the border tribe among my own people."

The narrator is the persona or aspect of the author's self who relates the story. Strange as this seems, the I who tells a story is distinct from the character who lived the story. The narrator has more perspective, more information, more language, and knows how the story will end. The I who tells a story is distinct from the living, breathing author. Narrators are created, two-dimensional personas with their own *created* personalities. Just as we must develop characters on the page, we must work to introduce and develop narrators.

This is as true for omniscient narration as it is for first-person narration. All writers shape the lens through which readers will see the action, using our sensibilities, values, insights—in other words, a distinct voice—so the reader feels the dynamic between the story's content and the presence for whom the story matters. This presence is perhaps most obvious when seen in comparison. From Louise Erdrich's *Love Medicine*:

The morning before Easter Sunday, June Kashpaw was walking down the clogged main street of oil boomtown

Williston, North Dakota, killing time before the noon bus arrived that would take her home. She was a long-legged Chippewa woman, aged hard in every way except how she moved. Probably it was the way she moved, easy as a young girl on slim hard legs, that caught the eye of the man who rapped at her from inside the window of the Rigger Bar.

From Jane Austen's *Sense and Sensibility*:

The family of Dashwood had been long settled in Sussex. Their estate was large, and their residence was at Norland Park, in the centre of their property, where, for many generations, they had lived in so respectable a manner, as to engage the general good opinion of their surrounding acquaintance.

From Gloria Naylor's *The Women of Brewster Place*:

Brewster Place was the bastard child of several clandestine meetings between the alderman of the sixth district and the managing director of Unico Realty Company. The latter needed to remove the police chief of the sixth district because he was too honest to take bribes and so had persisted in harassing the gambling houses the director owned. In turn, the alderman wanted the realty company to build their new shopping center on his cousin's property in the northern section of town. They came together, propositioned, bargained, and slowly worked out the consummation of their respective desires. As an afterthought, they agreed to erect four double-housing units on some worthless land in the badly crowded district. This would help to abate the expected protests from the Irish community over the police chief's dismissal; and since the city would underwrite the costs, and the alderman could use the construction to support his bid for mayor in the next election, it would importune neither man. And so in a damp, smoke-filled room, Brewster Place was conceived.

What does each narrator observe? Why? With what sensibility? Each omniscient narrator's presence is unique, with a lens tinted by personality, values, interests, and so on. The narrator uncovers insights, makes links between scenes, and generally provides a container for the story's events. Whereas characters inhabit specific time and place, a narrator needn't. A narrator can see universals and draw connections.

For memoirists, identifying a narrator persona can feel liberating. Your present-day self can step forward to comment on the story. The distance between the character self and the narrator self can contribute to your story's tension. Readers wonder, "How did the author get from there to here?" and read on to find out. The narrator can reflect, make meaning, give context, and relate a metastory to encompass the main action. This discourse between the past and the present, the self you were and the self you've become, is in fact a defining attribute of memoir.

Whether the narrator self shows up in creative nonfiction is the author's artistic choice. Likewise in first person fiction, where the I can be main character or narrator or both. Fiction writers can create this same effect in close third-person narratives by moving through time, portraying an older character remembering and being influenced by past events. Including a narrator or older perspective gives us the option to articulate why the story is being told and what meaning can be gleaned from it. Not including the narrator or older perspective immerses our readers in an experience, related without interruption.

Why are these choices significant? The many possible relationships between character and narrator within a story illuminate the many possible relationships between author and subject matter. What's your unique relationship? Represent it with your craft choices.

Common Pitfalls for Creative Nonfiction and Autobiographical Fiction

- *Overidentification with the I on the page*. When beginning writers write the word *I*, they conflate character, narrator, and author into a single identity. Who can blame them? Yet revision (and maturity as a writer) comes by developing a two-dimensional persona and sustaining a paradox: The I on the page both is and isn't the author. The I is a representation the author shapes. Writers have an obligation to be honest. But to write with integrity, we also must own the limitations of printed matter. We *always* craft a persona when we write the word *I*.

  Exercise: *Write a character sketch of your character self or your narrator self or both. What makes each unique? What characteristics of these personas are essential to your story? How might you convey these characteristics early in your manuscript?*

- *Early drafts that summarize*. Some beginning writers initially avoid the character self, thereby also avoiding the hard truths that details reveal. The narrator is so prominent, readers never experience the lived story. Such drafts read like journal entries; they rarely include scenes.

Exercise: *Choose a critical moment in your story—the introduction of conflict or an instant of transformation. In present tense, create a scene of this moment. Show it like a movie without any interpretation from your narrator self.*

- *Early drafts that are locked in the character self.* Just because you or your character didn't have the language at age four to describe thoughts and feelings doesn't mean they're not part of the story. What a younger self doesn't understand exists in lovely tension with what the older self now knows. Likewise with experiences that make us numb; emotions and awareness about emotions may come later but they are still part of our experience.

Exercise: *In scenes where your character lacked language or awareness, try zooming out to the narrator's point of view: "At the time I didn't know . . ." "Only years later would I come to see . . ." Write these reflections, as clumsy as they may seem. Then consider: Can you reveal these thoughts and feelings covertly in the scene? Might you want to include a more graceful rendering in your manuscript?*

- *The amorphous "we."* Readers need a specific pair of shoes to walk around in. Remember to describe your *particular* experience of groupthink.

Exercise: *In your notebook, ask why you chose third person plural in this passage. How did or do you know what others were think-*

ing or feeling? Can you show this in the scene? In revision, be sure to attend to your character's bodily experience. What did you see, smell, taste, hear, feel? What did you think?

- *Stating the obvious.* Good reflective writing contributes new insights to the narration. If your reflections simply *tell* what you've already *shown*, cut them.

  Exercise: *Underline all the exposition in your draft. Then ask of each passage: Does this move the story forward or retrace my steps?*

Exercises

Identifying Character and Narrator in Memoir

Consider a small memory in your draft or relevant to your project—preferably not a recent event. Don't look at your draft.

- *Write this scene in present tense. This is your character self.*

- *Without looking at this first draft, briefly rewrite the scene using a close past tense. Change the tense without adding any perspective. The protagonist of the story remains your character self in past tense.*

- *Rewrite it once more, this time beginning with your present-day self. "When I think of my childhood today, this moment stands out . . ." Allow this narrator voice to color the story and interject freely.*

- *Note the emergence of the narrator self in this last draft. The character inhabits the scene; the narrator reflects on the scene.*

If distinguishing between the character self and the narrator self is difficult, write all past events in the past tense and all present reflections in the present tense. You can always play with tense in later drafts.

Take a Stand

My partner, a dancer, recommends this exercise: Strike a posture that embodies your author self. Linger there, noting any sensations that arise. Then assume a posture for your narrator. How is it different or similar? Finally, find a posture for your character. As you write, let the sensations of these postures inform your voice.

Point of View in Fiction

Answer these questions about your draft (with thanks to Janet Burroway):

- Who tells the story? *A narrator or character? How would you describe this voice? Is there anyone better suited to relate this story?*

- To whom? *Often fiction's audience is general, but narrators can also directly address other characters or themselves or God, and these imagined audiences influence the narration. Carefully consider your narrator's audience.*

- Why? *Explore your narrator's need to tell this story.*

- In what form? *Is this simply a story? Or is it a collection of letters, a journal, a monologue, a plea bargain? Is there a form that might better serve your narrator's needs?*

- At what distance? *Has time passed or has physical distance come between the story's events and its narration? How psychically intimate or detached is the reader's experience of the characters? Might changing the narrative distance increase your story's tension?*

- With what limitations? *Is the narrator reliable or not? How does this serve your story?*

Practicing Respect and Compassion

For your readers to engage with your story, they must to some degree identify with the characters. As an author, you treat your readers with respect and compassion when you respect and feel compassion for your characters—along with many other contradictory emotions. In your notebook, explore the ways you do and don't respect each character in your story. Explore what makes your heart reach out to each character.

Seeing through the Character's Eyes

The novelist Charles Johnson says this about John Gardner's teaching: "To write well, for Gardner, is to obliterate for the duration of your fiction your own pettiness, to surrender your prejudices in order to seize another man's way of seeing—his truth, the way the world appears to him, then faithfully present it in the story." If revision is reseeing, one important perspective to take is your character's.

Draw a Venn diagram. In one circle list your attributes, attitudes, beliefs, strengths and weaknesses; in the other list your character's. Place the characteristics you both share in the middle, where the circles overlap. Creative nonfiction writers can do this exercise with characters other than themselves or with the character of the younger self.

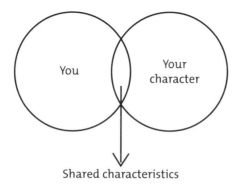

Shared characteristics

Control versus Release in Fiction

We've all heard what Vladimir Nabokov calls "that trite little whimsy about characters getting out of hand." That a character might take its author on a wild ride tickles our common fancy. In reality, characters can *and* do *make their wills known, but only in the midst of the author's many conscious choices. Nabokov called his characters his "galley slaves."*

I suggest a practice of both exerting your own ideas and being receptive to your characters' emergence. Plan your characters' attributes, delineate their histories, deliberately explore their personalities, plot out their desires. And then dialogue with them. What do they want for themselves? For the narrative? At times allow them autonomy; at others take control.

Exercising Your Voice

Voice is the narrator's personality expressed in language. Just like singers whose body shape and life experience and number of cigarettes smoked all determine a unique voice, we writers can do nothing about the nature of our voice. It's a given. Our history, personality, and values all contribute to the timbre of our words. Practice—sheer quantity—helps our written voice better represent our inner voice. But we can never step outside it.

I grew up singing in church, and well into adulthood my voice retained a clear boy's soprano quality. Then I began lessons with a Ukrainian American instructor who specialized in the raucous, nasal, full-bodied singing of Eastern Europe. Now I can yip and kuln and project. My voice is the same but it's been exercised. I've learned new tricks.

Writers can also widen our voice's range. We can take on different tones—bitter, inquisitive, curmudgeonly, bright. We can try different attributes: scholarly, childish, motherly; or styles: jazzlike riffing, deductive reasoning, stream of consciousness, intimate, formal. A seasoned writer with awareness of voice chooses how to use it rather than assuming that the voice of the first draft was inevitable.

This is why writers must read voraciously. We shouldn't fear the influences of other voices; we should greedily consume them. One way to expand the range of our voice is to imitate others.

The principal purpose of voice is to show the narrator's or character's relationship to the material. A unique lens illuminates a subject; a persona makes particular meaning of and responds emotionally to events. The more a narrator's or character's perspective colors the content, the richer the reader's experience.

Voice manifests itself in authors' styles—the choices they make with diction, syntax, pacing, tone, rhythm, paragraphing, and the like. Such linguistic techniques consciously and unconsciously create an overall effect: a unique voice. Lest you despair of contributing something new to the vast world of letters, consider Lynn Sharon

Schwartz's observation: "The only new thing under the sun is the sound of another voice."

Exercise

Imitative Writing

Deliberately immerse yourself in the works of a master writer whose prose is significantly different from your own. (I especially recommend imitating Virginia Woolf, James Joyce, Ernest Hemingway, Sandra Cisneros, and M. Scott Momaday for their distinctive voices.) From reading, move directly to the page. Using your own subject matter, write a paragraph in this author's style.

Reflecting In and On Your Stories

These days in creative circles expository or reflective writing is much maligned. But the "show, don't tell" dictum often results in stories with no guiding philosophy, no exploration of values—no deliberate thought on the part of the writer. Yes, *showing* creates a visceral experience for the reader. Yes, *telling* can be dull, didactic, and off-putting. But a stimulating story has action *and* depth, dynamic characters *and* moral exploration. Writers need to inhabit the interior life of our stories.

Characters are absorbed in themselves and in a moment in time. Authors and their distant narrators, on the other hand, have the advantage of hindsight and the capacity to contextualize events, anticipate consequences, and make patterns of meaning. Exercising this capacity is essential. "When writers remain ignorant of who they are at the moment of writing," writes Vivian Gornick, "that is, when they are pulled around . . . by motives they can neither identify accurately nor struggle to resolve—the work, more often than not, will prove either false or severely limited." We must know, or sense, or at least seek what our stories mean. Reflective work is often the only way to unify the inner story, that subterranean realm of ache and revelation, with the outer story.

Because we rarely see such connections in a first draft, fully exercising this reflective muscle is the work of revision. The goal of reflection is to move beyond our impassioned, distorted relationship to our material and instead see it directly, simply. This is at its core a contemplative practice—the ongoing effort of sidestepping the small self in service of the true Self. When we conflate ourselves with the character on the page or disavow any connection whatsoever, we are too close for perspective. But with practice we learn to hold a difficult paradox: We simultaneously are and are not our characters. Likewise, our early love—infatuation—is distorted by our eagerness to divide or deny what we see. **We love our *idea* of the person or project, but not yet the reality. With time and effort and intention, we can love the story for itself**.

The reflective voice is the prose writer's tool for gaining the perspective needed to achieve wholeness.

The project notebook once again is a place to muck around in broad, contextual, philosophical, and psychological questions. "From the mud a lotus," the Buddhists say. The lotus for writers is consciousness of our story's inner life. We see our story for what it is.

As you grow aware of your thoughts and feelings about a story, you can make deliberate decisions about whether to include these in the manuscript. At some point every writer needs to ask whether an overt narrator will serve the story, and if so, how. Instead of heeding the "show, don't tell" rule, try this advice: **Show first, then tell—if necessary**.[6] Write the scene. Figure out what you think about the scene—why it matters. Then challenge yourself: Can you *show* these insights? If so, fold them into the scene. If not, consider including the narrator's perspective.

Exercise

Show, Then Tell (if Necessary)

Underline all the exposition in your draft. Then ask of each passage: Can I show this in my scene without naming it overtly?

The Reflective Voice

How does the reflective voice work? Let's look at some examples, beginning with Mary McCarthy's *A Catholic Girlhood*:

> The fear of appearing ridiculous first entered my life, as a governing motive, during my second year in the convent. Up to then, a desire for prominence had decided many of my actions and, in fact, still persisted. But in the eighth grade, I became aware of mockery and perceived that I could not seek prominence without attracting laughter. Other people could, but I couldn't. This laughter was proceeding,

---

6   "Show first, then tell—if necessary" is a great policy when drafting and revising. It's not a hard-and-fast rule for the final product. A strong declaration from the narrator can be an effective lead.

not from my classmates, but from the girls of the class just above me, in particular from two boon companions, Elinor Heffernan and Mary Harty, a clownish pair—oddly assorted in size and shape, as teams of clowns generally are, one short, plump, and baby-faced, the other tall, lean, and owlish—who entertained the high-school department by calling attention to the oddities of the younger girls. . . .

It was just at this time, too, that I found myself in a perfectly absurd situation, a very private one, which made me live, from month to month, in horror of discovery. I had waked up one morning, in my convent room, to find a few small spots of blood on my sheet; I had somehow scratched a trifling cut on one of my legs and opened it during the night. I wondered what to do about this.

Note in the first paragraph the authoritative, knowledgeable tone of the narrator. Using adult language and insights, she summarizes and interprets events from her childhood. Her narrative perspective colors how we think about Elinor and Mary. She creates portraits of her characters before we see them in action.

I include the second paragraph because it shows McCarthy transitioning from that distant narrative point of view into a scene. The adult narrator tells us that her childhood situation is "absurd"; she's still interpreting. But then she leaves interpretation behind and we zoom in on Mary, the character, who wonders what to do about blood on her sheets. McCarthy segues smoothly between both perspectives throughout the story:

But precisely the same impasse confronted me when I was summoned to [Mother Superior's] office at recess-time. *I* talked about my cut, and *she* talked about becoming a woman. It was rather like a round, in which she was singing "Scotland's burning, Scotland's burning," and I was singing "Pour on water, pour on water." Neither of us could hear the other, or, rather, I could hear her, but she could not hear me.

The distanced narrator makes a connection between that frustrating moment and the childhood round; the comparison helps her readers experience the scene's tension.

Here's another example, this time from Bernard Cooper's *Truth Serum.*

Like most children, I once thought it possible to divide the world into male and female columns. Blue/Pink. Roosters/Hens. Trousers/Skirts. Such divisions were easy, not to mention comforting, for they simplified matter into compatible pairs. But there also existed a vast range of things that didn't fit neatly into either camp: clocks, milk, telephones, grass. There were nights I fell into a fitful sleep while trying to sex the world correctly.

Nothing typified the realms of male and female as clearly as my parents' walk-in closets. Home alone for any length of time, I always found my way inside them. I could stare at my parents' clothes for hours, grateful for the stillness, haunting the very heart of their privacy.

The overhead light in my father's closet was a bare bulb.

Again, note the transition from exposition into scene. The reflective voice allows Cooper to elaborate on his childhood mindset—one that's familiar to us—and so before he's begun his story about the closets (where he cross-dresses, an experience with which his reader might be less familiar) he has invited us into his childhood conundrum. He moves from the narrator's wide-angle lens to a close-up of the character. Here is his transition back out:

> A makeup mirror above the dressing table invited my self-absorption. Sound was muffled. Time slowed. It seemed as if nothing bad could happen as long as I stayed within those walls.
>
> Though I'd never been discovered in my mother's closet, my parents knew that I was drawn toward girlish things—dolls and jump rope and jewelry—as well as to the games and preoccupations that were expected of a boy.

Note how the reflective voice works like connective tissue, interpreting events and tying them to the story's heartbeat. When authors choose to include the reflective voice, they do so not because scenes don't speak for themselves—they always should—but because the author wishes them to serve some other purpose as well. In this case, Cooper sheds light on the permeable boundaries between the sexes and the hurtful impact of cultural norms on a child.

Memoirists and novelists writing about trauma are especially well served by an overt narrator. When a writer uses the present as a vantage point for examining the past, both writer and reader know that, however horrific past events may be, the narrator has survived. For those afraid that writing will retraumatize them, this narrative distance acts as a safe haven. Forays back in time (to, say, the six-year-old self) will make both writer and reader feel vulnerable. But a narrator stable and sane enough to write provides a home base. Therapists call this a *durable object*—someone (a parent, a therapist) who says, "You can't annihilate me; I'm here for you." A durable narrator makes possible the relating of memories that might otherwise be too painful.

In writing that is more immediate—an event that happened yesterday, for example, and any writing in the present tense—the character self conflates with the narrator self and reflection can occur without interrupting the scene. Take this passage from Mark Doty's *Heaven's Coast*. Out on a dog walk, Doty spots a wounded seal on a low rise of sand.

> The seal raises his head and barks and makes a noise like a hiss of warning; my worry for it is mixed with wondering what those teeth are capable of. . . . At the edge of the tidal stream it looks back to us, then slips into the water. It's no less awkward in three inches of water than it is on sand, but as soon as it reaches a foot-deep stretch of sea it's gloriously fluid, like a heron taking to air; what was compromised and lurching is suddenly capable of splendid and effortless motion.
>
> A body that was wounded sits stranded, incapacitated. Gone into another element, that same being takes gorgeous, ready flight. I am filled, entirely, with the image of my wounded lover leaping from his body, blossoming into some welcoming, other realm. Is it that I am in that porous state of grief, a heated psychic condition in which everything becomes metaphor?

In this passage the narrator, who makes meaning of events by writing about them, and the character, who was out on a walk, seem one and the same. The present tense is not literal—Doty isn't writing while he walks. Rather, it is a technique that invites the reader simultaneously into both scene and reflection.

We can also conflate character and narrator in the past tense, as in Virginia Woolf's "The Death of the Moth":

> It flashed upon me that [the moth] was having difficulties; he could no longer raise himself; his legs struggled vainly. But, as I stretched out a pencil, meaning to help him to right himself, it came over me that the failure and awkwardness were the approach of death. I laid the pencil down again.

In either past or present tense, when the character and narrator are united, action and reflection occur simultaneously.

These dynamics apply to first-person fiction as well. Note how the best novels defy the "show, don't tell" rule:

> It has seemed to me sometimes as though the Lord breathes on this poor gray ember of Creation and it turns to radiance—for a moment or a year or the span of a life. And then it sinks back into itself again, and to look at it no one would know it had anything to do with fire, or light. . . .Wherever you turn your eyes the world can shine like transfiguration. You don't have to bring a thing to it except a little willingness to see. Only, who could have the courage to see it?

Marilynne Robinson's *Gilead* devotes plenty of space to John Ames's existential ponderings, and this, I would argue, contributes to the novel's success. The reader inhabits Ames's affection for his home and parishioners, a pleasurable experience, as well as his old-fashioned theology, which is not so comfortable to a modern reader but which nonetheless undergirds the story's main conflict. From the start Ames expresses his urgency to relate this story— he wants his young son to know his aged father. We also suspect unconscious motivations for the narration that undercut Ames's stated intentions. This creates a lovely tension the reader is compelled to see to resolution.

Ames is a narrator for whom reflection is essential to his character—he is a pastor. But even the most thoughtless first-person narrators have a philosophy or cosmology from which their behavior arises, or that their behavior contradicts. Spoken or unspoken, reflective material remains a force in the story. As E. M. Forster writes,

> Daily life is practically composed of two lives—the life in time and the life by values—and our conduct reveals a double allegiance. 'I only saw her for five minutes, but it was worth it.' There you have both allegiances in a single sentence.

Meaning making, interpreting, ascertaining emotional import, applying values—the author must perform these duties to compose life on the page.

In third person, the narrator can directly address the inner story. In *Anna Karenina*, for example, Tolstoy chose a close third-person point of view that shifts between characters. Here we see the story through Kitty's eyes during her wedding to Levin:

On the day when, in the ballroom of the house in the Arbat, she had gone up to him in her brown dress and silently given herself to him, on that day there took place in her heart a complete rupture with her former life, and a completely new, different, and quite unknown life began for her, though in reality her old life was still going on. Those six weeks had been the happiest and the most agonizing time for her. All her life, all her desires and hopes were concentrated on this one man, whom she still did not understand, to whom she was bound by a feeling which she understood even less than the man himself, a feeling that attracted her to him and at the same time repelled her, and yet all the time she went on living her former life.

The narrator tells readers what Kitty recognizes as well as what she doesn't. How can she reconcile her contradictory feelings? We are as interested in the narrator—Kitty's vantage on the world—as we are in the narrative. Joan Silber calls this "fiction of consciousness."

At times fiction writers create a narrator persona who directly addresses the reader. Take this example from Arundhati Roy's *The God of Small Things*:

When they made love he was offended by her eyes. They behaved as though they belonged to someone else. . . .

He was exasperated because he didn't know what that look *meant*. He put it somewhere between indifference and despair. He didn't know that in some places . . . various kinds of despair competed for primacy. And that *personal* despair could never be desperate enough. That something happened when personal turmoil dropped by at the way-side shrine of the vast, violent, circling, driving, ridiculous, insane, unfeasible, public turmoil of a nation.

The omniscient narrator has perspective; she offers the reader information that illuminates her characters and increases tension: We now see what the character cannot. The reflective voice acts as a dynamic presence in the story.

Fiction writers have the option to create unreliable narrators, people like Nabokov's Humbert Humbert, who interpret events to suit their own ends, or Huckleberry Finn, whose perspective is flawed because of youth, and readers are delighted to inhabit a skewed or screwy outlook. This is also possible but rare in creative nonfiction. All human beings are unreliable. Despite our best intentions, the realities of a moment will conflict with our most genuine attempts to relate the truth. All literature plays with this discomfiting phenomenon.

One contemporary short story illustrating this is Andrew Bomback's "Deeper into Movies," a first-person account of a medical student who copes with emotional stress by transposing reality into a mental movie. He begins working with Monty, an African-American teenager who is dying of sickle cell anemia. As Monty's illness progresses, the narrator becomes less and less reliable. He gives Monty a romance, a jazz musician father, a bully rival. What is true and what is movie? Periodically, however, the narrator relates conversations with his preceptor in which he reports on his work with Monty. Here's an example where we catch the narrator lying.

"Okay," the psychiatrist says. "Anything else that came up in your interview?"

"Umm," I say, thinking, "not really. He did mention one thing that was interesting. He said he sometimes pictures himself in a movie."

"Explain that to me," the psychiatrist says.

"Well, he said sometimes he'll kind of fall out of himself, like watch himself as if he's part of a movie."

"Okay, I think I get it. That's a distancing mechanism. It's a form of denial. He's not the one who's suffering from this disease, he's not the one who's going to die. It's someone else, some movie character. That's a good point to put in your write-up of him. He's pretty advanced in terms of defense. He's protecting himself."

"Okay," I say, writing the psychiatrist's words down on a pad of paper.

"Did he really say that?" the psychiatrist asks.

"Sure. Why?"

"Maybe *you* said that."

"No, Monty said that."

"I was just making sure."

When a narrator is unreliable, the reader gets great satisfaction from deducing the truth about a situation through other characters and hints planted within scenes by the author. Behind the narrator's words we sense an author who knows better. How? We are deliberately made to distrust the narrator; the story hints at a reality beyond the presented details.

When should we zoom in on our character and when zoom out to our narrator's reflections? When should our verb tense reflect "reality" and when can we play with it? Which chronology, past or present, will best ground the reader? Should my narrator be reliable or not? Answers come only with experimentation while we ask, "What best serves my story's heartbeat?" The narrator's persona and reflective voice are tools authors use to create effect and meaning. They bow to a greater purpose. They work for the story's soul.

Tips: Advantages and Risks of Including the Narrator's Reflections

ADVANTAGES

- The narrator can overtly state the motivation for telling this story—thus answering the "So what?" question.

- The author can easily zoom in and out of scenes.

- The author can transition easily through time.

- The author can give language to languageless experiences. An adult narrator can be aware of what the child character couldn't recognize or feel what the emotionally numb character could not experience.

- The narrator can make meaning of experiences, calling attention to the inner story.

- The reflective voice can ease transitions and serve as connective glue.

- The distance between character and narrator can create tension or mystery. How did the narrator get from there to here?

- The disconnect between an unreliable narrator and the related events can create an exciting tension.

- The author can summarize ideas or time. Summaries done well augment and connect scenes.

RISKS

- *Telling* language stimulates the mind rather than the body. It's more difficult for readers to absorb.

- It's easy to lapse into summary that diminishes the narrative.

- The narrator voice can be dull, didactic, or journal-like—not welcoming to the reader.

- Whenever the narrator interjects, chronology is breached. Reflections done poorly steal the reader's surprise.

- The reflective voice can remove a story's subtlety.

- Building the reader's trust can prove more difficult. Scenes give the reader a direct experience; reflection asks the reader to trust the narrator's judgment.

- It's difficult to craft a stimulating and artful reflective voice.

A Few Words on Didacticism

Many of us write because we're fired up by some cause. This passion ignites us but can limit our willingness to see the subject from new angles. An author's single-minded agenda steals the life from characters; it clamps blinders on the plot and makes the prose preachy. When writers know what they want to say before they write, the result is what John Gardner calls "first-class propaganda."

Unfortunately, a fear of being didactic inhibits many American writers from tackling the social issues of our day. Contemporary literature that explores identity politics or institutional injustices or social ills often gets pigeonholed by publishers and sidelined by reviewers, who are quick to dismiss such work as having an agenda. As a result, contemporary American literature tends toward the narcissistic and myopic. **Writing that intentionally avoids social issues or ethical questions also conveys a message—that we aren't responsible for addressing injustice, that we can remain neutral in the face of evil**.

The young adult author Mitali Perkins freed me from this trap. "It's the nature of a story to have a moral," she said. "Stories that don't work because they're didactic are bad stories." Rather than deny any passion we feel for the political, environmental, religious, and social issues of our times, we writers need to harness it and ride it deep into our stories. Good stories hold complexity, contradiction, and surprise. What makes a literary work *moral*, John Gardner writes, is the author's willingness "to be changed by the process of telling the story."

> True art is *by its nature* moral. We recognize true art by its careful, thoroughly honest search for and analysis of values. It is not didactic because, instead of teaching by authority and force, it explores, open-mindedly, to learn what it should teach.

As we revise, we shed our assumptions, ask fresh questions, embrace paradox, and discover new meaning. We move from a state of knowing to not knowing, from a closed to an open heart, and in the process serve both our cause and our story. **Thus revision moves us from *moralistic* writing to *moral* writing**.

Reflection's Healing Work

Most early drafts focus on the personal and relational elements of a story. In revision we can remember the personal and public history, social movements, cultural values, technological advances, systemic ills, economic class, and myriad factors that make us who we or our imagined characters are. Authors must examine their stories in a historical, political, social, environmental, philosophical context. Why *this* story at *this* moment in time? By deepening the context, we make the story accessible to a broader readership. Such reflective work can appear overtly with the narrator's comments or covertly in structure, voice, or content selection. But appear it must.

When memoirists bring forward their two selves—the younger, character self and the narrating self who makes meaning—we achieve a unity on the page that is impossible elsewhere. We accept our contradictions, our ambiguities. We straddle the distance of growth. We identify what is unchanging. Likewise, when fiction writers take a collection of ornery, conflicted characters, set them in motion in circumstances we find curious, and form a wholeness there, a complete story, we are in fact working with the many aspects of our personality, subtly but powerfully affecting inner transformation. "No character is without philosophical function," John Gardner writes. **As authors, we not only tolerate the coexistence of our many selves, we also create a space where they function harmoniously. This is extraordinary work with ramifications beyond the personal sphere**.

Exercises

Balancing Reflection

If the first version of your story contains very little reflection from the narrator, try rewriting with a heavy narrative lens. Tell your reader up front why you're writing this story now, or why your narrator is telling it. If exposition makes you uncomfortable, remember that you can harvest the insights it brings, reshape your scene accordingly, and cut it later.

If your first version contains a lot of reflection, try rewriting without this voice, zooming in on your character's story.

Assessing Balance

Read through your draft, using one color to mark all the places where you've zoomed your lens down to your character and another to mark all the places where an older narrator is speaking. Ask: Is there balance between my two points of view across the manuscript? Do I ever use the narrator's reflection to avoid showing in scenes? Where might my story be strengthened by focusing in on the character? Are there any scenes about which I'm unsure what I think or feel? Where might this story benefit from more narrator reflection?

The Narrator's Self-Portrait

If your story uses a personified narrator, write a portrait of this person. For creative nonfiction writers: Who are you today, especially in relationship to the story you're telling? For fiction writers: Who is your narrator at the time of the story's telling? What of your narrator's values, personality traits, and dimensions of voice (humor, gravity, informality, formality, and so forth) might you bring to bear on your subject?

The Author Self

Periodically I step back from my work to ask, "Who am I as an author?" Here are some questions I find helpful:

- *If stories are able to shift the world a small degree, in what direction do I want it shifted? What do I most want to create for myself and for our world? How does my current story contribute to that bigger vision?*

- *What values do I want to live by? Does my work reflect these values?*

- *Have I been faithful to the story I am working on? Have I served it? By creating this story, what else—principles, values—am I serving?*

- *How does this project bring me joy? Is this joy evident on the page?*

- *What am I gaining through this project? Why? How might I harness this gain for my reader?*

- *In what ways is this story bigger or wiser than I am? How is this story challenging me to grow? Why might this story be presenting me with this challenge right now?*

Because I believe that, intentionally or unintentionally, literature influences readers, I also ask:

- *How would I like my story to impact my readers? Why? By what means would I like this to happen? How is it currently happening in my draft?*

- *How do I understand my role as a writer in society? In what ways do I hope my work shapes our culture?*

CHAPTER NINE

Strengthening Movement

Readers want a journey. Sure, we're curious about your recovery from addiction or your character's flirtation with suicide or the impact of immigration on a family. Sure, we want to know what happened. But we're more interested in the ramifications of these events—how were those involved changed? We want to trace this change so *we* might be changed. We want to be transported from one way of being into another, and to emerge different, however slightly. We read to be moved.

Movement is fundamental to literature. Writers are often surprised to learn that essays needn't make a point. An essay can ask a question, interrogate it, and arrive at a more lucid articulation of the question. What makes an essay succeed is *movement*. In essays, movement happens in the realm of ideas; in poetry, movement happens emotionally or aesthetically; in fiction or memoir, movement happens within and between characters, through events. Change defines stories. The questions "What is the story about?" and "What changed?" result in the same answer. Without change, there is no story.

E. M. Forster refines this idea. A story, he says, is "a narrative of events arranged in their time sequence. A plot is also a narrative of events, the emphasis falling on causality. 'The king died, and then the queen died,' is a story. 'The king died, and then the queen died of grief,' is a plot. . . . If it is in a story we say, 'and then?' If it is in a plot we ask, 'why?'" When the storyteller explores emotional connections and disconnections between people and events and the resulting changes, we get a plot—the force that compels a reader to turn pages. "When 'nothing happens' in a story," Janet Burroway says, "it is because we fail to sense the causal relation between what happens first and what happens next. When something does 'happen,' it is because the resolution of a short story or a novel describes a change in the character's life, an effect of the events that have gone before." A story works when events transform people, for good or ill, and the reader intuits why.

For this reason, **much of the work of revision is identifying and amplifying transformation**. What real changes occur? Where? Usually the external events that affect characters are easy to identify: the cancer, the avalanche, the divorce, the fiftieth birthday. These touchstones in the physical world are essential to good stories because they ground readers; they help us embody the character and immerse us in the flow of time. Internal changes are harder to realize. What are the subtle shifts in thought and emotion that influence characters' actions or the narrator's reflections?

Jonathan Franzen's character Sylvia from *The Corrections* describes a hidden movement fundamental to human experience and thus essential to stories.

When the event, the big change in your life, is simply an insight—isn't that a strange thing? That absolutely nothing changes except that you see things differently and you're less fearful and less anxious and generally stronger as a result: isn't it amazing that a completely invisible thing in your head can feel realer than anything you've experienced before? You see things more clearly and you know that you're seeing them more clearly.

Both layers—the outer and the inner—need sharpening in revision. A narrative comprised entirely of outer story reads like an action film, all plot and no character. Too much outer story frequently leaves readers asking, "So what?"

A narrative comprised entirely of the inner story is also unsatisfying. A student once handed me a hundred pages of spiritual visions she'd recorded that were utterly unreadable; they had no foothold in the specifics of her life. Go too far into the realm of the intellect and you've got academic writing, with no grounded story. Too much emphasis on the narrator's or character's transformation reads like a journal, self-absorbed and impenetrable. We're whole human beings with sexual longings and aching bones and troubled families. Instances of action and interaction give the interior journey traction.

In my experience, most writers have little trouble with the outer story. Something *happened* to ourselves or our characters; that's what compels us to write. But illuminating the inner story proves reliably challenging. Beginning writers assume that a reader will intuit internal changes simply by following external events, but this is rarely the case. Writers must *craft* the reader's experience; it *never* happens by default. We move the inner story forward by developing our themes.

Transformation in Theme and Plot

Rarely do I find formulas helpful in the creative process, but here is one that works. Every story can be broken into three parts: before, during, and after. Consider diet ads that show a frumpy middle-aged woman side by side with her buff, slender, post diet self. Implicit in the placement of these pictures is a story: She was overweight, she followed the diet, and now she looks fabulous! "Before" and "after" measure the change.

Each miniscule movement in a story and every grand transfiguration across a book pivots from *before* to *after*. In revision you can effectively intensify your plot by highlighting beginning and ending states and punching up the moments of change.

Before

A foundational part of every good story is the setup. Remember Rudyard Kipling's *Just So Stories*? To learn how the camel got its hump, we first must know it originally lacked one. Or Genesis: "Now the earth was formless and empty, darkness was over the surface of the deep, and the Spirit of God was hovering over the waters." We must first hear about formlessness and darkness before we can appreciate God's astounding proclamation, "Let there be light!"

"Surprise depends on expectation," Peter Turchi writes. "If we have no expectations, there are no surprises." As obvious as this seems, setup is often the most challenging part of a story. Our characters have vast personal histories from which we pull material relevant to the changes they'll experience in the story. Often we're not aware of a character's or our readers' expectations until after we've written the story.

I recommend exploring these questions to uncover *before* material:

- What history makes this moment significant?

- What expectations did I or my character bring to this moment? What expectations might my reader bring to this moment?

- What is at stake for me as a character or for my main character?

- What is at stake for me as a narrator? Or what is at stake for my story's narrator?

- What is at stake for me as an author?

Once you've responded to these questions, identify a scene that illustrates your main character before the transformation. The elements at play during moments of change take their significance from the story's history. Good openings drop the reader into a scene that forms the context for the character's change.

During

The actual moment of change is almost always action packed. Stay grounded in the external story, giving space to relational dynamics, thoughts, actions, description, and dialogue. Trust physical details to reveal the inner story. Remember that a character's thoughts and feelings within a scene are a critical part of *showing* the scene; they are not the narrator's reflection. Questions worth asking about your moment of change are:

- What happened?

- What was the agent of change?

- How do the stakes get raised during the story's action?

After

The significance of a story—the answer to "So what?"—resides in the consequences of change. A transformation is rendered worthless if it's not played out in events, thoughts, beliefs, and relationships. Again, from Janet Burroway, "Conflict ends with a significant and permanent change—which is the definition, in fiction, of a resolution." To find the locus of transformation ask yourself these questions:

- What changed?

- What were the consequences of this change?

- What meaning do I or does my character make from this change?

Then see if you can identify a scene that illustrates these consequences, especially in contrast with your *before* scene.

The consequences of change needn't be positive, wise, or moral. Just as an essay doesn't have to answer the question it poses, transformation in story can be in any direction so long as it *moves*. Once I worked with a memoirist who had a strong theological agenda for his story. Midway through writing it his mother died, throwing him into a faith crisis. Without a definitive answer to his questions about God, he assumed his project was in shambles. It wasn't. Uncertainty is a worthy landing place for a journey so long as it begins elsewhere.

Delving into the consequences of a change often kicks up new information about the nature of the change. Say I'm writing the story of the fire that destroyed all my belongings. When I explore the fire's aftermath—the smoldering books, the melted jewelry—I realize my grief is not for the objects so much as the human relationships they represented. Thus I have new information to bring back to the piece's beginning. Only those objects that show relationships bear weight—the heather-blue afghan my grandmother knit for my twelfth birthday, for instance; with Grandma in New York and me in Minnesota, the afghan had been my way of remembering her love. A month after it burned, a package arrived with a new one, knitted at terrific speed. We often don't know where significance resides in our story until we land at the end. Only then can we plant those details up front to prepare our readers.

Over a longer story, each moment of change becomes the starting place—the *before*—for the next. Change builds. When nothing happens in a story, the author has not tended these tiny gradations of transformation.

The external elements that show causality between the beginning, middle, and end are a story's plot. The internal elements—a story's emotional life—comprise its themes. The theme that acts as the single, unifying lynchpin is the story's heartbeat. We can work across entire manuscripts by considering the inner and outer stories in before, during, and after stages, we can work within individual chapters or scenes, and we can work within individual moments. Identifying and augmenting change gives stories momentum.

Exercises

Sketching Change

Choose a small scene in your larger project. Read it, then draw a timeline in three parts: "Before," "During," and "After." Above the line, list elements of the outer story: What events, objects, and characters are critical to the story's movement? Below the line, identify the corresponding inner story: What changed inside the characters (emotions, thoughts, beliefs) or between characters (relationships) because of these external events?

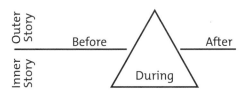

Now draw a similar timeline for your entire plot. What qualities comprise your character before and after the events of your story? What comprises the most significant cause of change?

This tool helps you identify the external causes of change and the internal movement of your story.

Before and After Portraits

Brainstorm five to ten details, moments, or scenes that might illustrate who you were or who your character was before *the central action of your story. Then create a portrait of this character. Can you locate this portrait within a particular moment in a scene?*

Do the same after *the events of your story. Brainstorm five to ten details, moments, or scenes. Create a portrait, then locate this portrait within a scene.*

You can do this exercise for an entire project or for a chapter or scene. Be sure to look at transformation in minor characters as well.

Expanding the "During"

Locate what you believe to be a critical instant of change in your story. Then choose three places in that passage to expand—one to give physical, bodily sensations, one to enter your character's thoughts or feelings, and one to delve into more detail on the setting. Linger.

Tracing Movement—the Lollypop Exercise

On a large sheet of paper, sketch a rough outline of your outer and inner stories like this:

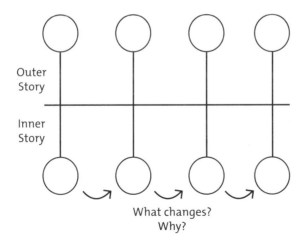

In the lollypops above the line, identify the main external events of your narrative—or in the case of an essay, the landmarks in the exploration of your idea. In the lollypops below the line, identify the corresponding inner story. What's happening below the surface, in the emotional, spiritual, intellectual, and relational realms? You may want to create several layers of lollypops here as a way to trace various themes. Then articulate the movement from one lollypop to the next. What changes? Why? Have you shown this movement in your manuscript? If one or more themes stay static across a chunk of text, revisit the text. Can you deepen the exploration of this theme?

Embodying Movement

Consider your story's plot. Move across a large space (your living room, a backyard) in a way that represents the nature of the story's unfolding events.

Then consider the story's inner life—its movement in thought, feeling, or relationship. Cross the space again, this time representing the story's internal movement. How are the two similar or different? What of your physical movement is or is not represented on the page?

Character Motivation

Stories grow out of a character's desires. In the before *part of your story, what does your main character want? Why? What's the origin of this desire? How does your character manifest this wanting? How might you amplify this desire?*

What stands in your character's way? Why? How might you strengthen your depiction of these obstacles?

How does your character's desire stay consistent across your story? How does it change? What of this desire is satisfied at the end? What isn't? What else is resolved, perhaps unexpectedly?

Connective Tissue

Take the deadest part of your story (usually in the transitions between scenes or thoughts) that is nonetheless essential. Imbue it with significance. Beef up the themes or drama or language. Make it the best moment in the story.

Thematic Development

Underneath all literature lies an implicit belief: We can give our lives shape and meaning. The fractured bits can be made whole. Nothing is lost or worthless. As my MFA advisor told me after a barn fire destroyed all my writing, "You have material, woman!" Stories are redemptive because they hold many paradoxical parts in a single container. *Shrada*, the Sanskrit word used for both "imagination" and "faith," literally means "the power to hold into one." Making stories is an act of faithful imagination. **As human beings, we long for unity. As writers, we intuit that writing helps us find it**.

But our stories first show their brokenness. We write random scenes with no sense of connection, or we write in strict chronological order, distressed by the dullness of recorded events. When a scene arrives, it raises reams of new questions and demands that other scenes be written. Characters appear with no seeming purpose. We grow attached to chunks of smart reflections but don't know how to transition into or out of them. Eventually we're swamped. In the face of so many disjointed pages, it's easy to despair. Not only have we *not* found unity, we've also made matters worse by using such a disorderly process.

In my experience, disorder is the necessary precursor to unity. Writing is like making stained glass windows; you gather the broken pieces, perhaps break some more, and only then solder together a cohesive image. Disconnected as our stories seem, they nonetheless contain unifying elements. Each of us has a unique and complete personhood; despite shortcomings and contradictions we are each whole, and therefore our stories can be as well. Whether we believe it or not, themes exist within our lives that bind the disparate parts of our work together. These themes are the questions that flummox you year after year, the faults that plague you, the longings that have driven you since childhood. These themes reside in your being, and they appear, like it or not, in your written work.

Working with themes, metaphors, and symbols—that is, listening deeply to what's unknown and unknowable in your story—opens the passage between the life of the spirit and the exterior. "Though we do not wholly believe it yet," James Baldwin writes in *Nobody Knows My Name*, "the interior life is a real life, and the intangible dreams of people have a tangible effect on the world." Certainly they have a tangible effect on our creations. What begins as a relentless sequence of events or a haphazard collection of fragments becomes a *story*, with purpose, unity, and movement. Working thematically is a way of nourishing the interior life—of ourselves, our art, and our readers.

When I ask students to identify themes in their work, they frequently give single word answers: Love. Motherhood. Home. While these answers may be accurate, they are not helpful. "The meaning of fiction is not abstract meaning but experienced meaning," as

Flannery O'Connor so practically describes it. Think of themes as explorations. How might I fight racism with all I've got *and* accept life as it is? Why does my character avoid confrontation? What makes a house into a home? Themes are the plot's inner life. They are the path by which particular experiences illuminate universal truths. The more clearly we identify our stake in each theme—why we care—the easier the theme is to develop.

The word *thema* in Greek means "what is laid down." I grew up a mile from a restored colonial farm and mill in the Hudson Valley. The summer after seventh grade I volunteered there as the weaver's apprentice. I wore a bonnet and bodice, milked the cow, carded and spun wool, and learned to weave. The loom filled an entire room; the beater was the size of a roof beam. I slipped the shuttle back and forth, watching the homespun wool gradually fill the warp with color. I pulled the great beam forward and beat each pass-through into place.

If drafting is carding the wool and early revision is "spinning a yarn," only deep into rewriting will you have vision to warp the loom—that is, to set the fiber so patterns will emerge when you begin weaving. Here you say, "The essence of my story is *such and such*; you will see it *here* and *here*." The scene that occurs on page three will be remembered on page sixty, will influence the character on page one hundred, and will reverberate under my climax. The ideas that appear within the first fifty pages will grow increasingly complex. Here you develop the through lines that bind your story's various parts. Here you refer back to earlier scenes and bring your digressive elements home.

Thematic work helps create a cloth with texture, pattern, and purpose. Consider themes in music: A short melody becomes the subject of a musical composition. Variations build on that melody. New melodies get introduced for contrast. Themes are recurring, unifying subjects or ideas. Thematic development distinguishes memoir from autobiography—it's what makes nonfiction creative. It is the maturation of a story's inner life.

Consider Frank Baum's *The Wonderful Wizard of Oz*. Kansas is bleak and, despite being well loved by her aunt and uncle, Dorothy wishes to be elsewhere. When the tornado strikes, her longing to return home pulls her through Oz. Along the way, the Scarecrow, Tin Woodman, and Cowardly Lion also ache for attributes of themselves they assume to be missing. As they encounter hardship, they each unknowingly manifest these attributes. Baum's story asks the questions, What is home? How do we find it? He answers with the story itself: Home is a quality we carry within us. We must leave home to find it.

Unity exists within every heartfelt story. We must trust it and seek it. "If the writer looks over his story carefully, again and again, reading aloud, his whole soul as tense as any stalking beast, he will begin, inevitably, to discover odd connections, strange and seemingly inexplicable repetitions," John Gardner writes. "In art repetition is always a signal, intentional or not, and when the moral artist finds in his work some such accident of language . . . he refuses to rest until he has somehow understood—or can emotionally confirm —the accident." These "accidents" are the dots we connect to see the larger picture.

When you read through your mass of pages, look for those threads that crop up across broad chunks of prose. Make a list. Draw flowcharts that trace the movement of emotions or ideas from scene to scene. What does your story explore? What questions does it ask? How do these themes change or deepen from beginning to end? How might you augment these changes? What is the magnetic stream, as Dinty Moore calls it, that runs throughout, drawing every word into its field? "In all this process," writes Kim Stafford, "the most enticing experience for me is the discovery of the thread, the second story, the background coherence, the thing I don't know until I do. Until this happens, life is random; after this happens, life is mysterious." **Whereas movement in plot lends a story its sense of adventure, thematic movement gives it meaning.** Finding emotional patterns hiding within and across your story is exhilarating—perhaps revision's most gratifying surprise.

Exercises

Themes in Life, Themes in Art

List five themes—grand questions or puzzles or truisms—from your life. Choose one that's evident in your project. What's your earliest memory relating to this theme? Write it. What happened in the last week related to this theme? Write that. Then journal in response to these memories. How might they inform your project?

Mapping Themes

Make a list of themes central to your manuscript. Give each a color.

Then create a representation of your story's progression from beginning to end. Map out the content of your draft on a big piece of paper or use sticky notes across a wall to summarize chunks of text. With your colors, mark when themes appear in your story. Then stand back. Where are certain themes prominent? Where do themes disappear? Where might you pull them forward?

Also trace how each theme evolves over the course of the story. It's not enough for "motherhood" to appear here, here, and here; your investigation of motherhood must move.

Reenter your manuscript, generating new passages and highlighting content that supports the development of your themes.

Motifs

Once you've developed your themes, you can do the fun work of pulling forward your story's motifs. A motif is a repeated figure in a design; in literature, motifs are the recurring images, references, and anecdotes that undergird your themes. Like your themes, motifs are already present but dormant in your text. Revision brings them alive.

Let's look at three examples from Patricia Hampl's *The Florist's Daughter*. The first is quite small: Hampl refers to F. Scott Fitzgerald throughout her narrative. Hampl's memoir haunts "Old St. Paul," and so her great love of Fitzgerald's work colors the setting and exposes the narrator's literary obsession. Fitzgerald never becomes more than a passing reference (although certainly Hampl thought of his work when describing the people in the upper crust world who purchased her father's flowers), but his name is like a bell rung periodically throughout the story. The reader thinks, "Oh yes! Here we are again."

The second example is a photograph Hampl describes in her opening pages—her young parents at a picnic. Periodically she returns to the image, using it as a window into her parents' early lives. When her mother's increasing bitterness baffles her father, Hampl refers to this photo as a way to remind the reader of who her mother had been. The more Hampl revisits the image, the more iconic it becomes. The reader feels the story coming full circle.

Hampl tells us early on that her uncle Frankie died a tragic death at the St. Paul brewery. Each time she mentions Frankie, we learn a bit more of the story—how he died, what his funeral procession was like, how his family mourned him. An anecdote that she could have related in two consecutive pages unfolds over two hundred. Frankie becomes a touchstone for the reader; we sense Hampl milking this tiny drama for all its worth. In a book that has precious little plot, Frankie pulls readers along.

Please note the potential binding power of such bits. Motifs contribute significantly to a story's unity. The more windows writers open onto this unity, the more alive our reader's experience.

Exercise

Finding and Developing Motifs

Make a list of images and peripheral anecdotes that appear in your draft. Circle those with energy—that is, they intrigue you or elicit some emotional reaction. For each of these, ask yourself these questions:

- *Where else might I plant this motif?*

- *How might I parse this motif across my manuscript?*

- *What else does this motif symbolize? (Try engaging it in dialogue.)*

- *Is there any place I can hint at this motif without showing it overtly?*

For those motifs you did not circle, consider what work they perform. Should they be amplified or cut?

Beginnings and Endings

We read from beginning to end, so it seems logical that we'd write that way too. Get the beginning right, then move forward, yes? In practice, however, starting at the start frequently feels grueling and can leave writers mired. Rarely do writers begin with material that will ultimately become their beginning. Beginnings often fall into place last. In other words, the reader's chronology is a poor guide for a writer's process.

If we don't know what a story is about until deep into revision, we can't possibly know how to begin. Beginnings must work hard, introducing characters, setting, conflict, the narrator's voice, and the emotional stake. Unless a galvanizing opening lands in your lap, I recommend not attempting the beginning until you're familiar with the bulk of your story.

Instead first write (and rewrite) those scenes and reflections you find most compelling. Use the Ouija board technique: Where in your project do you sense energy? Following curiosity is a good policy. Track down mystery; seek out the openings into tears and surprise. Compelling material makes us want to write. If we have nothing to learn from a scene, it's probably not worth writing. If we're involved in a scene, we usually have a stake in its outcome. Interest is a gauge worth heeding.[7]

Eventually you will have a mass of text in which you're highly invested. Only then is it productive to ask where the story begins.

---

7 Take note, however: Often a strong desire *not* to write a memory or scene can be a sign that it needs to be written. Strong emotional reactions to material are clues that your stake in the material is high.

Sometimes the story begins with the chronological beginning—the launch of the outer story. When this happens, revision requires that we trace the action forward, from beginning to end.

At other times the story begins at the beginning of an emotional quest, as with my student who wondered after her relative's funeral, "Who's next? And why is this happening to my family?" The quest begins at the funeral but takes the character back in time, to the reunion and other memories, then forward in time as more family members succumbed to their addictions. The author's emotional quest becomes the book's plot.

Stories can also begin with a lyrical moment that signals the heartbeat or with reflection that highlights the narrative voice in relationship with the subject matter, as in this passage from Zora Neale Hurston's *Their Eyes Were Watching God*:

> Ships at a distance have every man's wish on board. For some they come in with the tide. For others they sail forever on the horizon, never out of sight, never landing until the Watcher turns his eyes away in resignation, his dreams mocked to death by Time. That is the life of men.
>
> Now women forget all those things they don't want to remember, and remember everything they don't want to forget. The dream is the truth. Then they act and do things accordingly.

Or from *Speak Memory* by Vladimir Nabokov:

> The cradle rocks above an abyss, and common sense tells us

that our existence is but a brief crack of light between two eternities of darkness.

Or from Sandra Benitez's *A Place Where the Sea Remembers*:

> Remedios, *la curandera*, stands at the edge of the sea. The old healer is weary, a result, in part, of the countless times she has cocked her head in the direction of someone's story. Remedios knows the town's stories. Just as the sea, as their witness, knows them, too.

Note how these more poetic starts elicit a feeling or concept that hooks our curiosity: What does it mean to act as though the dream is the truth? If life is only a brief crack of light between two eternities of darkness, what sense will Nabokov make of his life? Is the sea weary of hearing stories too, or will Remedios find in the sea new energy for the town's stories?

Regardless, beginnings always introduce what's at stake. A reader enters a story asking, "So what?" and expects to trace an unfolding answer.

Endings, written early, can help steer a draft, but these too must be held lightly. We writers want to know and not know our endings, holding out for the possibility of something new. Endings needn't be conclusive; they needn't tie up all the loose threads nor land on a definitive solution to your mystery. "In your search for the right conclusion," Judith Barrington advises in *Writing the Memoir*, "don't fall prey to what has been called the 'triumphalist imperative,' which favors completion over complexity. Don't shortchange the reality of life in which significant events are rarely put aside in a moment of insight, but continue unfolding into the future." Remember: **Endings illuminate movement**. Readers need to land at a different place from where they began.

The best endings are organic, inevitable, and surprising. To find such an ending, I usually ask where the emotional journey arrives and how this can be illuminated in a scene.

Exercises

The Beginning of the Beginning, the Ending of the Ending

Where do you think your story begins? Write that beginning quickly. Then ask yourself: Where does this beginning begin? Write that story— and so on, until you've uncovered the emotional origin of your project.

This exercise also works for endings. Where do you think your story ends? Write it. Then ask: "What's the ending of this ending?" And so on.

Begin with the End

Reread your draft's ending. As an experiment, try beginning the piece again, only this time start with your final scene or reflections. Can you incorporate these insights and generate new ones by the time you complete this draft?

Begin with the Action

Where does your story's action begin? Start there and continue writing. Fold any preamble or backstory into the middle, or cut.

Begin with the Narrator

Ask yourself where your narrator's story begins. What instigated the writing or the exploring of this story? Begin with that scene and continue.

Generating Options

Once, when I was struggling with my novel's opening scene, a woman in my writing group suggested that I write five possible openings and choose the best. I thought this was preposterous. And then I did it—in fact I wrote ten—and finally found one that works. Sometimes we just need to generate possibilities.

If you're struggling with your opening or closing—or any other part of your story, for that matter—generate at least three alternatives and then choose the best.

Generating Beginnings

Use the suggestions below to generate seven new beginnings for your draft. Give each beginning five minutes; write quickly, moving past the opening sentence into the paragraph that follows. Then move on to the next suggestion.

1. *What is the question driving you to write this story? Write this question, using it as the opening sentence.*

2. *Fill in the blank: "Here is a _____(adjective) tale about _____(noun)." OR "What follows are _____(adjective) reflections on _____(noun)."*

3. *Write an opening sentence that is conversational, as though from the middle of a personal letter or phone conversation ("I never*

told you about the time . . ."; "*Don't tell your mother, but . . .*"; "*Just so you know . . .*"). *Don't worry about introducing the reader to your subject.*

4. *Begin with a description of the setting—where does your piece take place? What's happening in the environment around your story's opening action?*

5. *Begin with a date as your first sentence.*

6. *Begin with a verb or a command.*

7. *Begin with dialogue or interior dialogue.*

How do changes in your opening affect your voice? Your material? What works?

Comparing the Beginning to the End

Read the opening paragraphs of your draft, immediately followed by the draft's final paragraphs. Does the beginning forecast the ending? Does the piece's end respond directly to its start? How else do they or don't they speak to one another?

CHAPTER TEN

Finding Form

It's no coincidence that we use the word *body* when we talk about writing—the body of a novel, an author's body of work. Despite tangible evidence otherwise, a story is a living thing. It is the lovechild of a strange coupling between human and Mystery.

Because of this, the structure of creative work is discovered and supported, never imposed. Consider the architect's mantra, "Form follows function." A skyscraper exists because of land limitations, population density, and the nature of business relations; its properties (its purpose, its limitations) distinguish it from a bungalow or a Carnegie library. Likewise each piece of prose has a unique being—a focus, an exploration, a will, a heartbeat. At first we don't know whether our subject has sharp corners or curves, if it's solid or fluid, if it needs many compartments or just one. We discover the container that will hold our material as we discover the material.

How distressing! Particularly when writers set out on longer projects, we want—need, even—a structure to help us proceed. At the same time, nothing proves more deadly than a strict plan. An outline, storyboard, or any scheme serves us only so long as we hold it lightly and are willing to release it at first inspiration. When a student's sculpture wasn't working, Rodin advised him not to keep making little changes but rather drop it on the floor. What does it look like then?

Once again revision becomes a conversation with the story's will. We hypothesize a shape for our story, write a draft, and then respond to the shape that appears. At the beginning of a lecture on structure, my mentor Larry Sutin said, "I have become very worshipful of the writing voice and suspicious of all plans and intents." Writer Dan Kennedy describes the relationship between author and structure more whimsically:

> The work itself will start to take on shape and structure as it becomes its own thing. . . . The whole thing's bigger than you, you know, so you can relieve yourself of the burden of thinking you're in control of it. If you think you're driving, you're wrong. You're the passenger. As a matter of fact, you're not even riding shotgun—you're in the back seat, man. Come to think of it, you don't get to decide if the windows are up or the air conditioning's on, that's how much of a passenger you are in this thing. That's a truth and a trick.

Most writers fret about structure too much, too early. It's disconcerting not to know the story's shape. We imagine the perfect structure will act like a magic pot in a fairy tale, able to hold whatever we toss in. When I offer a class on structure, someone always asks, "Can you give us a lexicon of structures?" Really they're asking, "What pots can I choose from?" I offer a start:

- Chronological: narrative progressing from beginning to end, usually tracing an arc through building conflict to crisis to resolution

- Chronological with flashbacks

- Sandwich: first half of chronological front story, chronological backstory, second half of chronological front story

- Circling back: begin with the end, then proceed chronologically from the beginning

- Switchback structure: zigzag back and forth between time frames

- Geographical: movement through space determines story order

- Braided: two or three stories or explorations interwoven

- Collage: stand-alone shorts associatively placed to make a whole—what Madison Smartt Bell calls "modular design"

Knowing our options is good, but in fact as many possibilities exist as there are stories. Far more important is having the skills to listen to our material and bring forward its innate structure. "I work less than ever, it seems, at structuring what lies ahead in my work," writes Rick Bass, "and instead only plan my days, my external life, around the notion of staying in a rhythm or cycle of unknowingness." We must balance our intentions with receptivity.

Shopping for pots won't help. You're gestating a living creature.

Thoughts about organization begin to form as we generate and revise. I once worked with a memoirist who realized early on that all her stories related to her body. She decided to organize her material from head to toe, the same order in which she came into the world. While this structure may or may not work in a final draft, it helped her generate. The body became a checklist of stories. Once we complete a draft we need a structural theory to guide us through the next revision, and the next. The trick is to hold these theories loosely and to look beyond them to the intrinsic, emergent structure within our material. An undeveloped skeletal structure resides in an idea before we've even put pen to page; it grows and calcifies, unbeknownst to us, as the work develops.

Exercises

Drawing Structure

Virginia Woolf describes the structure of To the Lighthouse *in her journal as "two blocks joined by a corridor." Here's how she drew it:*

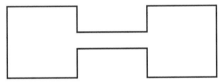

Consider your current draft. Create an image that represents its structure. You might draw blocks of text in relationship to one another. You might show the energetic movement of your story in colored lines or shapes. You might delineate the separate threads of your story.

Then play with the image. How else might it be arranged?

Flowchart

In your notebook or on a large sheet of paper, create a rough flowchart of your entire draft. This will give you a bird's-eye view, help you organize the significant chunks, and highlight the thematic movement. Then play. How else might the elements of your story flow?

Toolbox: Chronology

Stories, according to E. M. Forster, are narratives of events arranged in their time sequence, with the great advantage of making the audience want to know what happens next. Beginning, middle, end: The formula is as old as the hills, and for good reason. It works.

Yet what writer doesn't enjoy pushing against the natural order of events for art's sake? Deviance from the direct progression of time can surprise the reader, to extraordinary effect. Besides, playing with chronology is fun.

Here's the problem as I see it: First drafts, done well, are usually a chronological disaster. Our minds simply don't function consecutively. They leap hither and yon. They skitter off track at the least provocation, and this is a good thing. Only in a freewheeling mess will we find alarming connections and captivating revelations.[8] For this reason we should *never* constrain ourselves to chronology in a first

---

8 Writers of memoir take caution: The chronology that feels so obvious in our minds is mangled once we put pen to paper. What seems like a no-brainer is in fact a big challenge. A memory inspires us; we begin narrating the memory's external events. As we write, we realize that certain historical background is necessary to help the reader understand the significance of this event, so we backtrack. As we progress with our story, we gain new insights—into our motivation, into the various characters and their relationships, into this memory's significance—and interject these thoughts. Then we might relate this event to others that occurred later. Throughout, we're interjecting comments like "little did I know," allowing our narrator self to color the story. By the time we hit "save," we're mired in a chronological swamp—often without realizing it. Memory's skips and jumps feel natural. But when this process is represented on the page, it makes no sense to a fresh reader.

draft. We want to remain as open as possible to tears and surprise.

That said, these initial ventures through time are not as talented and literary as they first seem. The story order of an early draft is usually the result of whim, not deliberation. In revision we make deliberate choices.

How? First, figure out your true chronology. Take an unrestrained, leaping-and-jumping first draft and make a timeline of the events represented there. Be sure to identify the chronology of the interior world—the progression of emotions and thoughts—as well as the exterior. If you use a present-day narrator who resides at the end of the timeline, note where the narrator interjects. By comparing the actual progression of events to how our draft represents them, we gain two tools: perspective on our process, with all its hidden implications, and the slide rule of chronology. Both will guide revision.

The best writing fully welcomes the reader into the character's experience. I expect to meet my friend at the state fair; she never shows up, and I have a miserable time riding the Stratosphere alone. When I relate this story to my reader, the solitary ride has no emotional significance if I haven't first conveyed my expectation of company. To be carried along with a story, the reader needs the writer to re-create both the internal and the external worlds in their order of unfolding. If I wait until the end to divulge that I'm a reporter for the *Star Tribune* who's been asked to write a story about rides at the Midway and that I have a terror of heights, you have been cheated of my story's full drama.

Likewise, we must use care with descriptors. When I write, "Linny called me with shocking news," my narrator self breaches chronology. I've stolen my reader's surprise by interpreting the news before sharing it. Whereas if I blithely answer the phone and Linny, my Gucci-toting, well-heeled friend, says, "Elizabeth, take a seat"; if I then sit with my heart racing and hear the words, "I'm leaving corporate life to take vows at an Italian nunnery," I re-create the shock for my reader. A single word like *shocking* can interrupt our story's chronology and drain its drama. Be especially alert to lead sentences that summarize—"Our move to New Orleans was devastating"—and therefore steal surprise. All interjections from a present-day narrator should be made deliberately.

Only once we've been disciples of true chronology should we begin to break it. I like Larry Sutin's advice: Use chronology unless you have a good reason not to. We need chronology to invite readers into our story and carry them from beginning to end, from *before* through *during* to *after*. Only once we know the true progression of events and insights can we recognize reasons good enough to toy with their order.

Another way to think of this: Our content has certain strictures we must obey, but once we've heeded these strictures, we have tremendous leeway.

Exercises

Chronology

Read through your draft, making a list of all major anecdotes in your piece. Order them chronologically. If this entails rearranging, try rewriting your piece in this order. If you're inclined to break chronology, justify it in writing: What purpose does breaking chronology serve?

Chronology and the Narrator

Using a colored pen, mark all the text in your draft where your narrator self speaks. Be aware that the narrator interjects with single words as well as lengthy reflections. Every time the narrator intervenes in your story, your chronology has been breached. Evaluate each instance by asking, "Do I have a good reason to break chronology here? Does it detract from or serve the story?"

The Power-Through

Thanks to Liz Olds for this exercise: After you've amassed enough material for a book, step back and, in a single sitting, write your entire story in ten to twenty pages. This summary helps you sort out your chronology while forcing you to select the story's highlights. If an event wasn't worthy of your power-through, does it belong in your manuscript?

Take It Apart

If your draft tells multiple stories across the entire manuscript, try this exercise: Physically separate the different stories and read them con-

secutively. For instance, if your draft alternates between a front story and a backstory, or if your draft sandwiches one story within another, rearrange the pages so you can read the narratives consecutively. Do they make sense? Is each consistent in tense and voice? Do they balance one another in length or power or purpose? Do they speak to one another?

Emergent Structure

Generally a piece's structure makes itself known quite late in the project. Only after a writer discovers his intention, Stephen Dobyns says, "can the work be properly structured, can the selection and organization of the significant moments of time take place. The writer must know what piece of information to put first and why, what to put second and why, so that the whole work is governed by intention." Only rarely does a structural concept arrive *deus ex machina*. More often it evolves as the story evolves and as the author's knowledge of the story increases. After working on *Hannah, Delivered* for five years, after trying dozens of organizational ideas, I found that the material worked well in nine sections—a fortuitous number for a book about birth. The structure was so pleasing, I did a little victory dance. Two years later, I faced the unfortunate fact that the nine parts didn't serve the story. Out the window they went.

How do we recognize emergent structure? Structure in creative prose is influenced primarily by three forces—content, voice, and process.

How Content Shapes Form

One way to identify a piece's structure is by looking closely at the natural attributes of the content. This is a practice of seeing and reflecting *what is*. I once had a student who was writing a memoir about her brother serving a life sentence in a high-security federal prison in the Arizona desert. Razor-wire fences, locked doors, Plexiglas barriers, and limited phone access made connecting with her brother nearly impossible. Certain structures (for instance, a lyrical, fluid, or circular form) simply would not serve this story. The hard edges of her content will inevitably influence her structure, perhaps as disconnected anecdotes or abrupt transitions.

Contrast this with the novels of my friend who plays cello in an orchestra: Marcia's work includes soaring musical descriptions and associative meandering through memory. The lyrical quality of her content dictates a lyrical form, with long chapters dreamily floating backward and forward through time.

Your material has a nature from which you cannot deviate. The inherent qualities of each story suggest a particular form. Your job is to know the nature of your material. Fiction writers can shift their content's nature by, say, making a shy character outgoing or creating a world without gravity, but once they've established these elements they must remain faithful to them. If the character is indeed shy, an outgoing act goes against his personality and therefore adds tension to the story. This should be a deliberate choice on the part of the writer. Our characters must be consistently inconsistent; a world without gravity must obey its own laws.

Writing about water suggests a different structure than writing about elephants or nuclear missiles or marriage. Poets occasionally play with this literally in "shape" or "visual" poetry; thus a poem about breath might have space between short lines or a poem about birds might suggest flight with the placement of words. Prose writers have fewer visual tools at their disposal, but we can still experiment with the length of chapters or sections, story order, patterns of narration and reflection, the quality of transitions, text breaks, repetition of content or form, chapter and section titles, and other elements. We can make structural choices that mirror our content, thus *showing* with form.

Exercises

Inherent Structure

Fill in the blank and answer quickly, without much thought. If your book or piece of writing were a _____, what would it be?

- *Animal (dog, cat, monkey, bird, rabbit, lizard, other)*

- *Feature of the landscape (mountain, river, valley, lake, desert)*

- *Type of food (candy, vegetable, hamburger, ice cream)*

- *Type of building (skyrise, bungalow, Carnegie library, bunker)*

Now journal: Why? What do your answers reveal about the nature— and possible structure—of your piece?

The Nature of the Material

Write a list of twenty adjectives, adverbs, or phrases that describe your story's content. For example, if you're writing about the role popcorn has played in your life, you might list "abundant, astonishing, noisy, nourishing, buttery, addictive," and so on. If you're writing about a mother grieving a lost child, you might list "ache, absence, unrealized dreams, unwelcome transformation," and so on.

Then make two more lists: "Possible Structures" and "Impossible Structures." What forms might work for this material? What forms could never work? Try to include at least five in each list, being conscious of the reasons they might or might not succeed.

How Voice Shapes Form

As we explored earlier, voice reveals the author's or narrator's emotional, intellectual, bodily, and spiritual relationship to the story. In so doing, voice informs that piece's structure.

The terms *narrative, reflective*, and *lyrical* are usually used to describe different voices, but they're also helpful in uncovering the primary impetus behind our writing and thus its structural possibilities. I think of them as engines—the machinery that propels our work. The *narrative engine* is fueled by the question "What happens next?" As readers we turn the pages of a good narrative because we're compelled by the plot. The *reflective engine* is fueled by curiosity around an idea: What sense do I make of this? The plot we follow is a train of thought. The *lyrical engine* is fueled by contemplation. Reading lyrical work, we tunnel down into an emotion or moment or image.

See how these forms are rooted in the author's personality? They are different ways to solve a mystery. The sleuth's strengths and shortcomings and personal involvement determine the best approach.

Once again, *why* you write shapes *how* you write. Your stake in a project shines through your narrator's voice. What feeling is at the root of this manuscript? Describe it. Create a metaphor for it. Allow that feeling to speak. **Usually writing is born of some discomfort—an ache, a longing, a curiosity. The more aware we are of this discomfort, the better we can harness its energy. Our discomfort has shape.**

If you are driven to write because of what happened, real or imagined, chances are good your story will take a narrative form. Your main character stumbles on a dead body; shock ensues, and events unfold that further cloak that murder or bring it to light. Or your main character is in her house when a tornado strikes and lifts her into a strange world of munchkins, witches, and a yellow brick road. How will she get back to Kansas? Or your main character is a child living in poverty in Limerick, Ireland, with too many siblings and a drunk father. How will he survive? Plot, or the progression of events and their consequences for characters, determines the structure of most fiction and memoir. Beginning, middle, and end: A character lives through time, experiencing a sequence of events and their accumulating consequences.

If you're inclined to make meaning or find significance, your form is likely reflective. Personal essays, which approach a central mystery down a path of ideas, are our role model here. Take Lauren Slater's "Dr. Daedalus," a detailed profile of Joe Rosen, a renowned and eccentric plastic surgeon who wants to give people wings. "Rosen's ideas and aspirations, not to mention his anthrax concerns, go beyond what I am comfortable with, though I can't quite unearth the architecture of my concerns," Slater admits early in the essay. The unease driving Slater is twofold, born of the strangeness of Rosen's ideas and her inability to articulate why they're disconcerting. These mysteries power the essay's plot, which gets its structure from the progression of Slater's understanding.

If you have poetic inclinations and are interested in a more associative, aesthetic investigation of an experience, your form will be lyrical. Abigail Thomas's *Safekeeping* is a memoir made up of one-to-four page vignettes arranged associatively rather than chronologically. Their progression gives the reader a sense of memory's leaps and flashes and the author's deepening tenderness toward these broken moments. "Modular design," Madison Smartt Bell's term for lyrical form, "allows the writer to throw off the burden of chronology. . . . [It's] an attractive way to show relationships between events or people or motifs or themes which are not generated by sequences of cause and effect and so are somehow atemporal."

Only rarely does a work fit neatly into a single category. Most novels include moments of reflection and an undergirding study of an idea; most essays tell a story; all good prose at some point abandons time and place to revel in sensory or aesthetic experience, or asks the reader to draw emotional connections. The narrative, reflective, and lyrical modes are at everyone's disposal. But in any project only one form is central and thus structurally defining.

In her essay "Flying in the Middle of Art," Annie Dillard describes the antics of stunt pilot Dave Rahm: "Like any fine artist, he controlled the tension of the audience's longing. You desired, unwittingly, a certain kind of roll or climb, or a return to a certain portion of the air, and he fulfilled your hope slantingly, like a poet, or evaded it until you thought you would burst, and then fulfilled it surprisingly, so you gasped and cried out." How do we control "the tension of the audience's longing"? **Underneath any successful story resides the authentic longing of the author. We must locate this longing deep within our text and build everything, including our structure, from its passion.**

Exercise

Voice and Structure

Consider your stake in your project. What are your top three reasons for exploring this content? Write them down.

As best you're able, categorize these motivations as narrative (discovering the consequences of events, real or imagined), reflective (questing for meaning), or lyrical (unpacking an image or emotion). Which of these forces is dominant?

What do your primary motivations suggest about how to organize your material? For example, if you're interested in how past events determine a character's present decisions, this interest could suggest parallel, intersecting narratives. Or it might suggest a more lyrical structure that allows associative leaps through time.

If you're writing fiction, what do these motivations suggest about your narrative point of view? For example, novelists intrigued by how characters experience the same events differently might inhabit multiple first-person points of view (Michael Dorris's Yellow Raft on Blue Water *or Barbara Kingsolver's* The Poisonwood Bible*) or an omniscient narrator who dips into multiple characters' consciousnesses.*

How Process Shapes Form

I'm a tenderhearted gardener. When last year's cherry tomatoes reseed themselves, I don't have the heart to pull them out. So I end up with an abundance of late-ripening cherry tomatoes. What to do? Make sauce. But cherry tomatoes are a hassle to peel, even after blanching, so I choose the lazy route, slice them with skins on, and throw them in the pot. The resulting sauce is tasty but watery and swimming with skins.

"The way a thing is made controls and is inseparable from the whole meaning of it," writes Flannery O'Connor. Process shapes product. Our exuberance, laziness, playfulness, discipline, bull-headedness, kindness, skill, and other qualities play a part in the text we finally create. Just as my choice to give the cherry tomatoes room in the garden rather than planting good saucing Romas contributes to the quality of my spaghetti dinner, each choice we make in the course of writing contributes to the reader's experience. Even those decisions we reverse, I would argue, build up like layers of paint to affect the final, aesthetic read.

Of the factors that contribute to our final product's shape, process is the factor most often ignored and from which we can learn the most. Process is also where we have the most power to influence results.

I once worked with a memoirist who wanted to write about her father, who in his large extended family was the only one to survive the Holocaust. His grief and depression colored her childhood. She was adept at writing beautiful narrative chapters about periods of her life, and amassed 150 pages like this before realizing that these stories had deftly skirted her intended subject—her father. But when she tried to home in on him, she got stuck. "I just can't find my groove," she told me. "All I've got are these fragments."

I suggested she pay attention to her process. Instead of trying to construct long, chronological chapters, simply write fragments. At first, she told me, this felt awkward, but eventually the fragments took on life. Their form—fractured, brief—mirrored the nature of her relationship with her father. As of the last draft I saw, they were interspersed between the longer narrative chapters. Only by accommodating her process to the needs of the material did this writer find her form. I imagine Kathleen Norris made a similar discovery when she wrote *Dakota*. How to write about the weather, an influential part of Norris's "spiritual geography" and a culturally defining topic of conversation in the Dakotas? Short weather reports do the trick.

What *works*? What techniques squeeze the content out of you? When I was miserably single, I set out to write an essay about my ill-conceived belief that God intended me to be lonely. As I wrote, I realized that my sense of divine will was very much in flux. What I believed at the beginning of the essay changed by the time I reached the middle, making a theological muddle. So I set myself the task of writing periodic credos to help nail down my beliefs. These credos not only guided my process, they also became landmarks in the essay.

Forums like a revision journal or a writing group help us step out of the writing river to examine the state of our boat, the current, and the river's general direction. *How* are we getting where we're going? What's working? What's not? **Writing well requires a willingness to try many different means to an end**. The means that come naturally have real advantages, but so do various other learned techniques. We must be responsive to our material, changing our approach to suit its needs.

Recasting

I began this chapter by describing structure as a container, and I'm not alone—editors and agents use the term *recast* when seeking new forms for a story, as though content is bronze that can be melted and repoured. But the reality of revising structure is more complex. A story's form reveals the author's relationship to the subject matter, and this relationship evolves over time. "Revising story elements changes a story's meaning," David Michael Kaplan writes. "Revising story structure also changes its meaning. Conversely, seeing a new meaning in a story will necessitate revisions in its structure and elements." Unlike bronze casting, a new mold for a story changes the nature of its content.

This evolutionary muddle is, in fact, good. The writer's tears and surprises on the path to finding form contribute to the reader's experience. Readers consciously or unconsciously seek a sense of the story's shape. Form helps readers interpret a story; it lends a story meaning. "This is how we make sense of what we read," Peter Turchi explains; "we work to put the parts together. We expect to discover an intended whole." The writer's delight in arriving at the whole feeds the reader's delight.

Exercises

Process, Product, and the Map of Experience

Identify some activity from your daily life (other than writing) where the process becomes evident in the form. You might choose cooking, gardening, a craft, child-rearing, making a business agreement, and so on. Describe this activity. How does process contribute to a creation's form? Then examine this activity as an analogy for your writing.

Linking Process with Form

In your writer's journal, create three columns. In the first, list a dozen different writing projects you've completed. In addition to creative pieces, include holiday letters, school papers, reports for work, jour-

nals, *significant letters, e-mails, Facebook posts, and so on. In the second column, briefly describe your writing process for each project. What did you do first, second, third? How did you work? In the third column, reflect on how your process for each project influenced its final structure.*

Increasing Awareness of Process

In your writer's journal, either describe or draw a representation of your writing process thus far in your current project. What means have you used to get to this stage? Then reflect: Where would you like to take your project next? What means might best serve this next step? What means have you yet to try?

Get Physical

When your desk starts getting cluttered with old drafts of chapters, feedback from readers, paper napkins scrawled with new ideas, and pages of research, try organizing with a banker's box. Give each chapter or section of your book a labeled folder. Place in that folder only material that might inform your revision. This way you can access your material in reasonable amounts. Organizing your book physically, with a three-ring binder and divider tabs, can bring insight into its structure.

Toolbox: Playing with Structure

Here are some techniques for getting a bird's-eye view of a draft's structure so you can then imagine alternatives.

- For a short piece: Cut it into chunks, then rearrange them on the floor or a bulletin board. How else might you order this story?

- For a longer piece: Summarize chunks of text on index cards or sticky notes. First arrange them as your draft is arranged, and number them. Then arrange them chronologically and number them using a different color. Finally, play with the order.

- Outline your draft, articulating for each chunk of text both the outer and the inner stories.

- Diagram or map your draft. Images help us see and work with the entirety of our story. If your story is a flowchart, what is the movement? If your story is a landscape, where are the vistas, the deserts, the inns?

- Articulate the progression of your story. First, on a large sheet of paper draw "stepping stones" representing chunks of text or chapters or significant moments in the plot. Identify the outer and inner stories within each stepping stone, as shown in the illustration.

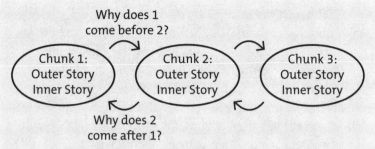

Then articulate why each chunk of text comes before another, and why after. If your explanation is chronology—your text follows the order in which the events occur—generate yet another reason. Just because things happened in a particular order doesn't mean they must be told in that order. More than one reason for artistic choices means more layers to the story.

- Draw the movement or energy or tension of the draft. This may be abstract art (using color or line) or musical notation (where are the crescendos? the rests? the repeats?). Are there alternatives to this movement that might better serve your story?

- Dance your draft. Represent the figurative movement of your draft by physically moving through a space. If you have an adventurous writing group, choreograph a short dance representation of your project. Afterward explore any tension, freedom, obstruction, beauty, and surprises that emerged for all participants.

"If it ain't broke, don't fix it." We humans prefer what's familiar. An early draft structure doesn't seem broken, so we don't want to tinker with it. Save the early draft and tinker with a copy, staying open to the possibility that your early structure may still be the best. Sketch out three alternative structures for your piece, all significantly different from your rough draft. Choose one that will stretch you as a writer and try it. What works? What doesn't? What did you learn that you might take back to your initial structure?

Late Revisions and Completion

CHAPTER ELEVEN

Adding by Subtraction

Something must die before something new can be born. This is what pastor and writer Nadia Bolz-Weber calls "spiritual physics." It's how the world works.

Recently I cut eighty pages from a polished, four-hundred-page draft of my novel. That's one-fifth of what I'd previously considered a complete book. What was in those pages? Scenes that slowed down the plot, unnecessary dialogue, whole paragraphs of exposition, and hundreds of extraneous words extracted from too-long sentences. Everything I cut was *not* the story. For example, I had written twenty pages of conflict around an insurance salesman; these pages were climactic, I thought, and illustrated the hardships all health-care workers endure within our insurance-governed medical system. But when I looked closely at the book's heartbeat, newly articulated, I was forced to admit that the exploits of the insurance industry did not support my exploration of faith and fear. I'd created this scene to serve my own agenda rather than to move my main character through her struggles.

After ten years of work on this novel, I am humbled by the volume of what I've written that is *not* my story. Perhaps other writers are more efficient; perhaps others can anticipate the heart of an emergent story or focus their work during the initial drafting or otherwise find shortcuts that don't shortchange the quality of their writing. I've yet to find an easier method. I generate years of notes and scenes and reflections, and then revise "until kingdom come," as my mother says. In the final stages, I'm a spring gardener—*hack that holly down to the ground; give that spirea a deep shave*. The story's lifeblood is trustworthy. If I'm ruthless now, it will flower when it's read.

"Good writers take out what mediocre writers leave in," playwright David Mamet once said. How do they know? Because inner stories are discovered, writers *don't* know until fairly late. We can't recognize which details *work* until we know what work they need to do. Then we see the proverbial darlings for what they are—boons to our egos, or red herrings—and get out the hatchet.

Once you have some clarity about your heartbeat, you can evaluate every theme, scene, character, detail, and digression for its efficacy.[9] Does it distract? Cut it. Does it distract but is necessary? Condense it. Does it distract but nonetheless haunts you? Dig deeper to find out why it's there.

These last elements I call Aunt Fannies. A colleague of mine wrote a gorgeous novel that included the main character's Aunt Fanny. Marcia wasn't sure what purpose Fanny served. Fanny had an affair, and she illuminated a central character's weaknesses, but

---

9   Philip Lopate's guidance on digressions is excellent: "The chief role of the digression is to amass all the dimensions of understanding that the essayist can accumulate by bringing in as many contexts as a problem or insight can sustain without overburdening it. The digression must wander off the point only to fulfill it."

she wasn't complicating the plot in any vital way. The story would have worked without her. When Marcia's agent suggested Aunt Fanny get the ax, Marcia dug in her heels; she interrogated Aunt Fanny about why she was in the story, and eventually got an answer. Aunt Fanny needed to become the catalyst for a climactic confrontation and the cause of another character's death. "I put the question into my mind," Marcia told me, "and it took several months before the answer came. When it did, it was a bolt from the blue. And then it seemed so obvious!" By listening to her character, Marcia recognized a new web of relational complexity.

Generally, however, **we do our best work of deepening and strengthening a heartbeat by eliminating all that doesn't serve it**. Refining a work is like using a colander to strain out what's no longer needed. What's left behind is pure story. Here again is that old spiritual practice of surrender. We know the story's soul shines through when pages of our work seem superfluous and we are willing to slough them off for the sake of that light.

Exercises

The Bare Bones

On a paper copy of your draft, highlight any text that is absolutely essential. You can work on a macrolevel, highlighting general scenes or passages that are crucial, or you can work on a microlevel, highlighting each word, but don't do both at once. Then give serious consideration to the unnecessary text. Can you cut it? Can you transform it to become essential?

Experimenting with Grief

Unlike loss in life, writers can test whether cutting text from their projects is worthwhile—that is, transformative. Choose a paragraph you'd consider eliminating, then cut it. What's lost? What's gained? Is your grief for the story's diminishment or the ego's?

CHAPTER TWELVE

Language

In the early stages of revision, we gain clarity about heartbeat, pump life into the story's organs and systems, and knit together bones that will help it stand upright. In the late stages we tend the text's cosmetics. Finally we know just enough about the story's essence to help it shine through the skin—the language.

This is a great policy—in the abstract. Early on, we don't always know which words or sentences are worthy of careful construction and when polishing language is really a distraction from the hard work of composing. Only much later will we see which passages are germane—a good reason to keep a repository for cut passages. Generally writers pay more attention to word choice, sentence structure, rhythm, and sound the closer they get to publication.

But writers can't help but attend to language from the get-go, perhaps because we derive so much pleasure from accurate, well-constructed sentences. On one extreme are writers who perfect each sentence before proceeding to the next. I don't recommend this method as it poses far too many opportunities to become mired. Attachment to polished sentences hinders our flexibility. Restructuring a book or lopping off a character are nigh impossible when all the sentences are beautiful.

On the other extreme are blessedly sloppy drafters who spew out text, trusting revision to tighten their prose. I know writers who, when unable to conjure up the right word, insert asterisks. The right word will come eventually. Preserving the flow of ideas is more important.

Most writers fall somewhere in between. We try to stay loose but can't help but consider the words. Luckily, language is quirky; just as a strong working title can give direction to a draft, the right word can unlock material. An accurate description can reveal a character's nature or the truth about a memory. Precision with language can elucidate unconscious motives. "Until you start practicing the language of the story, start hearing the music of the story, you can't learn what the story has to tell you," writes Tobias Wolff in Woodruff's *A Piece of Work*. Occasionally slowing or even stopping one's flow to deliberate over language can be beneficial.

Once more, writing asks us to walk the middle way between minute details and universal purpose. Staying alert to our motives keeps us on track. Is an early quest for accurate language motivated by genuine questions about the content? If so, our work with language reveals the heartbeat and is worth pursuing. Is our struggle for the right word motivated by concerns for the reader? Or an effort to represent ourselves well? Or to procrastinate? If so, postpone that work. Better to seek the core of the story first and polish the surface later.

Words Matter

Great premium is placed on language in our literary culture. Is it fresh? Is it witty? Does it dazzle? The question I wish reviewers and publishers would ask is "Is it true?" Readers need writers who name the vast diversities of reality with language that elucidates rather than obscures. The novelist Charles Johnson recommends writers use the Buddhists' Three Gates of Right Speech before they put their work into the world: Is it true? Is it necessary? Is it kind? **The word or image or metaphor that moves a reader's heart is beautiful because it's honest, needed, and life-giving**.

Truth, of course, is relative. But the truth I'm referring to isn't singular or objective; it's resonant, full of both mystery and fact. We've all had the experience of reading a passage that describes a familiar object or event in a way we've never considered but which feels absolutely right. Here are a few of my favorites—first, from Virginia Woolf's "The Death of the Moth":

> The rooks too were keeping one of their annual festivities; soaring round the tree tops until it looked as if a vast net with thousands of black knots in it had been cast up into the air; which, after a few moments sank slowly down upon the trees until every twig seemed to have a knot at the end of it. Then, suddenly, the net would be thrown into the air again in a wider circle this time, with the utmost clamour and vociferation, as though to be thrown into the air and settle slowly down upon the tree tops were a tremendously exciting experience.

Woolf's image of a knotted net is an accurate description of birds rising and returning to a tree. The comparison aids the reader; we see more clearly because of it. Both the image (quite ordinary) and the language (quite simple) help the reader experience this moment. The longest Latinate word in the passage—*vociferation*—is noisy, its sound imitating the clamor of birds. Nothing in this passage calls attention to the language or the author.

Unlike this passage from Zora Neale Hurston's *Their Eyes Were Watching God*, where attention-grabbing language serves the story:

> She was stretched on her back beneath the pear tree soaking in the alto chant of the visiting bees, the gold of the sun and the panting breath of the breeze when the inaudible voice came to her. She saw a dust-bearing bee sink into the sanctum of a bloom; the thousand sister-calyxes arch to meet the love embrace and the ecstatic shiver of the tree from root to tiniest branch creaming in every blossom and frothing with delight. So this was marriage! She had been summoned to behold a revelation. Then Janie felt a pain remorseless sweet that left her limp and languid.

Here words *do* demand our attention, but not for the sake of the author's self-aggrandizement. The extreme word choices—"panting breath," "sanctum of a bloom," "love embrace and the ecstatic shiver of the tree," "a pain remorseless sweet"—help us understand Janie's adolescent sentimentality. Janie knows extreme passion that is incongruent with her life's dull prospects. Inhabiting her point of view is intense, ecstatic, and memorable.

The truth revealed in these passages is dual. First, these authors name physical reality accurately and beautifully. They represent the facts on the page in a manner that is fresh and revealing. Second, they choose details that point through physical reality to some emotional, spiritual, relational, or psychological truth—the inner story. This happens during revision.

We can create resonant truth with expository language as well, although it is most effective if linked to narrative. Take this remarkable landing from "Notes of a Native Son," after James Baldwin's interlinked stories of his father's death, the Harlem race riots, and his own exploding fury after being refused service at a whites-only restaurant:

> It began to seem that one would have to hold in the mind forever two ideas which seemed to be in opposition. The first idea was acceptance, the acceptance, totally without rancor, of life as it is, and men as they are: in the light of this idea, it goes without saying that injustice is a commonplace. But this did not mean that one could be complacent, for the second idea was of equal power: that one must never, in one's own life, accept these injustices as commonplace but must fight them with all one's strength.

Abstract words rightly earned, placed well, and applied intelligently can make beautiful prose. Note how Baldwin's repetitions ring like bells. Note how, despite the complexity of these sentences' construction and the paradoxical nature of the ideas he's conveying, his words are quite plain. Above all, he wants to communicate. The integrity of his language mirrors the integrity of his struggle with racism.

The authors I respect most do not seek to impress; they seek to discover, to uncover, to name what *is*. Hemingway is famously quoted as advising himself, "All you have to do is write one true sentence. Write the truest sentence you know." A true, simple, declarative sentence unlocked Hemingway's work and kept him going. He never bothered to define truth; rather, he intuited it, and this intuition served him well. It's excellent advice: Write your truth, in your own true sentence.

Tips: Finding the Words

- Write quickly and plainly. As best as you can, use your natural language. Because you have an innately unique voice, your language will be fresh if you show up on the page.

- Reflect in a journal. Writing for no audience eliminates strain and self-consciousness from language. After remembering your natural voice, return to your manuscript.

- Research for accuracy. If you're having trouble finding the right word, return to the source, either in reality or in your imagination. Go to the place you're describing; dig out the photograph that inspired you; talk with someone who shares your character's accent. Think and feel deeply about your subject. Authentic language emerges from precise observation.

- When clichés appear, take note. Keep going if you're writing an early draft, but later return to these passages and ask yourself what this easy language hides. Clichés signal that we've taken on others' explanations of the world rather than discovering or inventing our own. They point to shallowness in thinking—an acceptable naming of reality rather than a naming that digs. Replace them.

- Read drafts aloud, record yourself reading and play it back, or have others read your drafts to you. Practice listening to your language without the impediment of text. What do you *hear* that you didn't *see*? Attend to the places where you or the reader stumbled.

- Beware of using quotations. "But so-and-so says it so much better!" my students protest. Quotations that replace the author's words are a crutch. Quotations work best as events in the narrative—for instance, as a character's encounter with a book or as inspiration in the narrator's thinking.

- Strive to serve the story and not some sense of writerly writing. Choose words that reveal, not conceal. Use the thesaurus to find accurate rather than fancy words. We usually know when we've designed a sentence to impress. Eliminate such prose.

- Use the dictionary. Whenever you are uncertain about a word's meaning or its implications, look it up. Know the origin and history of significant words in your story.

- With each crucial word choice or description, first ask yourself, is it true? Only then ask, is it fresh?

- Read Strunk and White's *Elements of Style* every few years. Their advice is spot-on and modeled by their language:

Omit needless words. Vigorous writing is concise. A sentence should contain no unnecessary words, a paragraph no unnecessary sentences, for the same reason that a drawing should have no unnecessary lines and a machine no unnecessary parts. This requires not that the writer make all sentences short, or avoid all detail and treat subjects only in outline, but that every word tell.

Exercises

Truth and Integrity in Language

In her memoir I Hear Voices, *Jean Faraca describes conversations the poet Donald Hall led with his students: "Did the poem ring true? . . . It was integrity we were testing, the poet's as well as the poem's. Beneath what was written on the page, we were learning to read ourselves, to unearth in the poem's encryption our own deep-seated dreams and fears." Ask these same questions about your language, especially in critical passages like beginnings, endings, and turning points:*

- *Does it ring true to reality as you understand it?*

- *Does it represent truths you believe in?*

- *Does it have integrity with the story's content?*

- *Do you maintain your integrity by using this language?*

Word Choice and Mood

Find a paragraph or passage in which you hope to convey a mood (anger, fear, levity, recklessness). Examine all your word choices in this passage, not just those that signify the mood. Can you shift the language so every word elicits this mood?

Verbs and Adverbs

Underline all the verbs in a paragraph of your writing. Star any accompanied by an adverb. Can you home in on the action more precisely and eliminate the adverbs? Can you augment the power of your verbs with more accurate choices?

Nouns and Adjectives

Underline all the nouns in a paragraph or two of your writing. Star any accompanied by an adjective. Can you find more precise nouns that show detail rather than summarizing? Can you make the adjectives unnecessary?

"Show" with Language

When tweaking language during the final stages of revision, strive for clarity. Language is meant to communicate. Sound, rhythm, pacing, word choice, sentence structure, punctuation, paragraphing —all stylistic choices—should convey the content. Language first and foremost should support the relationship between reader and subject matter. The best way for writers to achieve this is to choose language that supports *our* relationship with the subject.

Within the scope of clear language are many choices, and fine writers opt for words that *show* as well as *tell*. Beginning writers tend to think of *showing* as creating scenes, when in fact we can *show* with most craft choices. Word choice, punctuation, sentence structure, and paragraphing can and should be used deliberately to illuminate what's happening in the content. This is what makes expository writing lively, as Maxine Hong Kingston shows in *Woman Warrior*:

> Adultery is extravagance. Could people who hatch their own chicks and eat the embryos and the heads for delicacies and boil the fat in vinegar for party food, leaving only the gravel, eating even the gizzard lining—could such people engender a prodigal aunt?

This passage from Richard Rodriguez's "Late Victorians" illustrates how paragraphing can be effective:

> Four years ago on a Sunday in winter—a brilliant spring afternoon—I was jogging near Fort Point while overhead a young woman was, with difficulty, climbing over the railing of the Golden Gate Bridge. Holding down her skirt with one hand, with the other she waved to a startled spectator (the newspaper next day quoted a workman who was painting the bridge) before she stepped onto the sky.
>
> To land like a spilled purse at my feet.

Pacing communicates in this excerpt from *The House on Mango Street* by Sandra Cisneros:

> I am an ugly daughter. I am the one nobody comes for.
>
> Nenny says she won't wait her whole life for a husband to come and get her, that Minerva's sister left her mother's house by having a baby, but she doesn't want to go that way either. She wants things all her own, to pick and choose. Nenny has pretty eyes and it's easy to talk that way if you are pretty.
>
> My mother says when I get older my dusty hair will settle and my blouse will learn to stay clean, but I have decided not to grow up tame like the others who lay their necks on the threshold waiting for the ball and chain.
>
> In the movies there is always one with red red lips who is beautiful and cruel. She is the one who drives the men crazy and laughs them all away. Her power is her own. She will not give it away.

I have begun my own quiet war. Simple. Sure. I am one who leaves the table like a man, without putting back the chair or picking up the plate.

In *The Things They Carried*, Tim O'Brien's sentence structure conveys tension and personality:

"These six guys," he said, "they're pretty fried out by now, and one night they start hearing voices. Like at a cocktail party. That's what it sounds like, this big swank gook cocktail party somewhere out there in the fog. Music and chitchat and stuff. It's crazy, I know, but they hear the champagne corks. They hear the actual martini glasses. Real hoity-toity, all very civilized, except this isn't civilization. This is Nam."

And Pico Iyer demonstrates why punctuation is our friend in his essay "In Praise of the Comma":

Punctuation . . . gives us the human voice, and all the meanings that lie between the words. "You aren't young, are you?" loses its innocence when it loses the question mark. Every child knows the menace of a dropped apostrophe (the parent's "Don't do that" shifting into the more slowly enunciated "Do not do that"), and every believer, the ignominy of having his faith reduced to "faith." Add an exclamation point to "To be or not to be . . ." and the gloomy Dane has all the resolve he needs; add a comma, and the noble sobriety of "God save the Queen" becomes a cry of desperation bordering on double sacrilege.

Note how clarity trumps grammatical correctness in these examples. Even Strunk and White concede that certain situations require sentences to end with a preposition: "A claw hammer, not an ax, was the tool he murdered her with." "Murdered her with" is violent and broken; "with which he murdered her" weakens the impact. Giving the reader a visceral experience of our content is more effective than strict obedience to rules.

Whether readers are conscious of such choices is irrelevant. Readers *feel* language; emotional and bodily reactions affect the reading experience.

Without clarity of vision—without knowing what meaning we want to communicate—crafted language is mere flourish. This is yet another reason to postpone polishing language until the end, when we know what the work is about. Only then can we choose words, sentences, and paragraphs that serve the story's pulsing heartbeat, thus placing the story in living relationship with reader and world.

Exercises

Structure Sentences and Paragraphs for Arrival

Choose a sentence or paragraph from your draft that contains a surprise, insight, or point. Rewrite it. See if you can sustain suspense until the sentence's or paragraph's end. Here is an example from "Late Victorians" by Richard Rodriguez:

> *I have never looked for utopia on a map. Of course I believe in human advancement. I believe in medicine, in astrophysics, in washing machines. But my compass takes its cardinal point*

from tragedy. If I respond to the metaphor of spring, I never-theless learned, years ago, from my Mexican father, from my Irish nuns, to count on winter. The point of Eden for me, for us, is not approach but expulsion.

Sentence Structure Mirroring Action

Choose a moment of action in your draft. Rewrite it so the sentence structure reflects the energy of movement you're describing. Here's an example from "Modern Times" by Lawrence Weschler:

> *But, strangely, the image that really haunts me, and the one I just can't shake, is that of my colleague in the eerie glow of his Nexus console, calmly punching that set of keys, activating the machine—the machine silently humming away, survey-ing the veritable continents of information before it, instanta-neously targeting its quarry, yanking it out of the endless field and delivering it up to us whole. The surgical precision of the whole process.*

Sentence Structure Mirroring Content

Choose a moment in your draft where you hope to convey a signifi-cant experience or idea. Use the order of words, punctuation choices, rhythm, and sound to amplify this experience or idea. Here's an exam-ple from "Memory and Imagination" by Patricia Hampl:

> *I sometimes think of the reader as a cat, endlessly fastidi-ous, capable, by turns, of mordant indifference and riveted attention, luxurious, recumbent, and ever poised. Whereas*

*the writer is absolutely a dog, panting and moping, too eager
for an affectionate scratch behind the ears, lunging frantically
after any old stick thrown in the distance.*

Paragraphing

*Choose a climactic moment in your draft. Read it through. Then do
the following:*

1. *Identify a significant action in the scene. Can you demonstrate
   the nature of this action through the progression of sentences
   inside your paragraph, or by your paragraph breaks?*
2. *Identify a moment of tension in the scene. Can you demonstrate
   the nature of this tension by its placement inside a paragraph?*
3. *Consider the energy of this passage. How might your paragraph
   lengths and breaks mirror this energy? How might paragraphing
   complement the pacing of your story or reflections?*
4. *Where in the passage is a surprise or new insight? Try using a
   paragraph break to augment the experience of newness.*
5. *Try incorporating a single-sentence paragraph into your narration or reflection. How does this shift the pacing? The emphasis of
   the content?*
6. *Try writing an extra-long paragraph. How might this paragraph's
   length strengthen the reader's interest and augment the paragraph's content?*
7. *Rewrite a paragraph three times: first, opening with the climax;
   second, locating the climax in the paragraph's center; third, ending
   with the climax. How does the location of the climax affect the
   reader's experience?*

To What Effect?

Edgar Allen Poe believed the purpose of the short story was to create a single, unified effect. If the writer's "initial sentence tend not to the outbringing of this effect, then he has failed in his first step. In the whole composition, there should be no word written, of which the tendency, direct or indirect, is not to the one pre-established design." Does your opening sentence conjure your story's "effect" or heartbeat? How about your closing sentence? Point randomly to any sentence in the manuscript. How does this sentence support your story's unity?

Toolbox: When to Stop Revising

Most writers (myself included) assume our projects are finished prematurely. My first publisher asked that I rewrite my memoir using two time frames rather than three; executing this change took me a full year after the book had been accepted. When my agent took on *Hannah, Delivered*, we reworked it over four years. Writers' urgent desire to be done colors our sense of completion.

Therefore, like every other stage of writing, knowing when you're finished requires discernment. Toward the end of a project, when you receive a suggestion or an idea for revision, ask these questions before you proceed:

- Does the suggestion or idea feel right for the project?
- Does the change offer you the chance to learn something about your subject? Will you grow by continuing

to revise? Does this opportunity excite you, despite the effort it will entail?

- Does revising offer you the chance to learn about craft?
- Will the change help bring wholeness to the manuscript or within you?
- Will the change help your story land more solidly on the truth?

If you answer no to these questions, you're done. When there's no more room for the writer to be surprised, there's no reason to keep going. If you answer yes to any of these questions—if your project still has a grip on your heart, mind, or literary skill—then you are resisting the ongoing effort of writing. Resistance never ends. We need to be savvy about distinguishing ordinary resistance from the recognition that a piece is truly done.

How do we know when a work is complete? It feels balanced. It has integrity. For many writers, knowing when to stop revising is helped immensely by others' responses. Suggestions from readers you respect (writing coaches, writing groups, agents, editors) no longer ring your inner tuning fork.[10] Recommendations tend to contradict one another or be petty. Or you receive unanimous affirmation

---

10   Keep in mind that finding a publisher may or may not be a sign of arrival. Books that desperately need development get published daily, and remarkable, completed books are rejected all the time. Also remember that some agents and editors have a vested interest in seeing your work in print as soon as possible. Don't let their authority eclipse your own. Once again you must trust the story and the whisperings of your heart.

> that your work is finished. Usually at the end of a project, authors long to cut the umbilical cord and move their creative energy elsewhere. The well of tears and surprises is dry.

Perfectionism versus Wholeness

How do you know when to stop revising? Many writers fall into the trap of mistaking revision as a path to perfection; they revise perpetually as a tactic to avoid failure or success or to reach some imaginary pinnacle of artistic achievement.

Perfection punishes the soul; it is an elusive and damaging goal. Writing is much like the messy work of child-rearing. Your kid will never be perfect and there's no way in hell you'll ever be the perfect parent. Over time you come to accept your child's propensity to embarrass and amaze you. You do your darnedest to parent well. Even if your twentysomething isn't fully mature, he's able to function independently. Let him go.

There's no magic landing place for creative endeavors. In the Japanese aesthetic of *wabi-sabi*, all natural and human creations are considered incomplete. Because of this, *finished* is an arbitrarily designated moment on the artistic journey. The evolving sense of discovery and creation can continue beyond publication, as authors witness others' interactions with, and therefore get new insights into, the story. This can be cause for regret, certainly, but also great joy. I look back on my early work much as I do at photographs of my younger self. I might wince at the ugly glasses frames and awkward posture, but ultimately that younger self is worth celebrating and continues to offer gifts.

One of the most well-known examples of *wabi-sabi* is *kintsugi*, the Japanese art of fixing pottery with gold lacquer. Breakage and repair are understood to be a part of the object's history, and therefore beautiful. Stories are a form of *kintsugi*. The cracks contribute to an aesthetic unity. As Leonard Cohen sings, "There is a crack, a crack in everything. That's how the light gets in."

Our attempts at perfect offerings are doomed; only cracked offerings have real potential. The humblest reviser who dedicates years to the evolution of her manuscript, who is thorough in her research, and who receives the best editorial support will nonetheless overlook a clumsy sentence, a spelling error, or a character contradiction. She will hurt a family member's feelings. She will perpetuate an inaccurate stereotype. Her book, even if lauded and applauded, will in places make her wince. Precious few literary attempts ever achieve perfection. The Shakespeares among us are rare, and even Shakespeare's work is riddled with errors.

That said, when someone criticizes my work I almost never see "how the light gets in." I feel its shortcomings acutely and reenter the perfection trap, where only "good enough" work belongs between covers or ought to have been written at all. Worse yet, I'm tempted to assume that the inadequacy of my writing reflects my own inadequacies: *I* don't belong here either. When Mark Doty's sister read his memoir she told him, "The things you got wrong just make it that much more you." Ouch.

Conflating our value as persons with the value of our art is dangerous, even when the value is high. **Imperfect as we may be, we *do* belong here, and imperfect as our work may be, it belongs as well**. Everything is cracked. In a backhanded way, Doty's sister's comment was really a compliment. We want our art to be ultimately *of* our best selves, saturated through and through with our essence, because this makes it unique. We don't want our art to be a perfect, replicable beauty; rather, we want a human beauty that transcends asymmetries, blemishes, and defects. Just as good medicine seeks healing over a cure, goodness in art springs from wholeness rather than perfection.

Most of us are embarked on foolishly unachievable yet ultimately worthwhile projects. "What matters most in our lives is unsayable," Mark Doty says. "We've got to attempt to make meaning. . . . Of course it's impossible, but if we don't, we despair." Stories take shards of human experience and make them into a complete window. They don't fix wrongs, they don't solve problems, they don't offer false hope. They simply hold together what we cannot.

Perfection is impossible, but wholeness is within everyone's reach. We writers have to inhabit the uncomfortable paradox of our simultaneous brokenness and wholeness. Especially as we reach the end of a project, writers must work like mad to fix what we can and make peace with the project's shortcomings. **Completion requires compassion for all the ways we and our work have failed; it requires faith that the work holds both truth and beauty regardless.** The work is and we are "good enough."

CHAPTER THIRTEEN

The Word, the Self, and the World

We write, so many authors claim, to find out what we think. Personal discovery is woven into the effort of making literature. We also write for the love of it, and because we long to communicate the mysterious workings of our interiors with others. Art-making gives us life, broadens our understanding of creation, and invites us into the human community. It changes us.

Unfortunately, a rift exists in our culture between the practice of the literary craft and the very human lives of those who write. When writing teachers despair over how ineffective they are or cynically claim that writing can't be taught, I suspect they know their students must change for their writing to improve and don't know how to facilitate this transformation. The written word may be wiser than the human who wrote it, but never by much. To write stories that move readers, writers must be willing to move themselves *and* their work. They must become endlessly curious, keenly observant, dogged in their pursuit of truth, and disciplined in their practice. Our most influential teachers support the development of these qualities alongside literary skill.

Writing classes rarely address students' philosophies or personalities or emotional maturity directly; to do so would be inappropriate—too personal, and dangerous. A writing class is not group therapy. And yet the fear of getting personal fosters an environment that can dissociate writers from their material. When discussing a work in progress, many teachers instruct classes to critique craft rather than content—as though the two can be tweezed apart. The good advice to "show, don't tell" in stories has discouraged writers from thinking deeply. Too often in our classrooms and in society, art is not a means for full and effective engagement with life but rather an end in itself—a product to be bought and sold, which may or may not win the writer contests, popularity, or esteem. Such an approach to art serves the personal ego and a culture of competition, but is death-dealing, for both artist and society. For writers to never address the inextricable link between craft and the human creator is a mistake.

The good news is that writing *itself* invites us to become more curious, aware, reflective human beings. The way writing can transform us makes me think of liberal Christian theologian Marcus Borg's definition of salvation as "seeing anew." **There's always room for us to be "saved" by changing how we see, and any project can be "saved" if we're willing to look at it from a new angle**. A writer genuinely interested in improving her craft won't get far without also seeing—and therefore living in—the world afresh. A writer seeking personal growth through writing won't get far without developing his craft.

I work at the intersection of writing coaching and spiritual direction, supporting writers in the development of their work and in their efforts to live lives of intention, and I'm continually astounded by how a commitment to craft encourages spiritual growth. Consider the qualities necessary to the gestation of an idea: attentiveness with all the senses; deep listening to one's inner voice; the ability to heed one's creative impulses; the discipline to place one's inner world onto the page. And consider what's necessary to draft a piece of writing: tolerance of chaos and poor quality; uncertainty about the work's worth; physical and mental discomfort; reverence for one's own questions and ideas; trust in one's intuition; reliance on one's unique process; a healthy egotism.

The transformative power of writing continues beyond the journal and initial drafts into revision. We learn humility as we endure the messiness and length of the process; we learn patience with our continued imperfection. We let go of attachments. We come to see that, despite the glare of inspiration, we can be agents in shaping our work and the world. We learn to trust the deep well of revelation available within and beyond a project.

The mysterious work of honoring the story's will above our own is an act of service. As writers, we claim our desires; we trust them and act on them. At the same time, we surrender our desires to the subtle, quiet will that appears on the page. This call and response is instructive to anyone attempting to serve principles or beliefs beyond the whims of the ego. Likewise with the strictures of the craft: We discipline ourselves with the rules of writing well, then release any limitations they impose in service of the story's life.

When considering an audience, we learn to cut what does not give life to the story and expand what does. We practice humility as we take in others' feedback while staying centered in our vision. We learn the sacred art of hospitality, seeking connections between the small scope of our story and a bigger world—the pressing hurts and desires of people on the streets, the legacy of literature that precedes us, and the future we participate in making. We claim the power of the printed word. We trust our stories to influence public discourse. Our stories teach us to become more responsible citizens.

And when a piece nears completion, we recognize its wholeness, its sense of balance, and its life independent of us. We let it go. We exercise compassion, for ourselves and for the work, because the work will never entirely manifest our vision. Rejections ask us to be dogged; we exercise hope. We release our need for others' approval while remaining open to the likelihood that our work might need further development. We separate rejection from our own worth or the worth of our work. The publishing process requires endurance. Every author continues to grow after a work's publication, but this does not diminish the work's value. When others praise our writing, even this success must not sway us from our course. We practice staying faithful to what matters most.

And if we understand marketing to be part of the ongoing creative process, our printed work can build community. It can open dialogue, opportunities to connect with and learn from readers. Just as we were moved in the writing process, we can move our readers —even move our culture—with intention, effort, and humility.

Finally, in the fallow period between projects, we rest. The creative wellspring has limits; we need to renew ourselves with reading, dreaming, and quiet. The blank spaces between creative endeavors are rich and trustworthy sabbaths. Emptiness and dryness in the creative cycle yield dark but wondrous gifts.

This is what the writing practice looks like when it's an exercise of love.

I'm convinced that for our art to be influential we must fling the doors wide between selfhood and craft. Regardless of one's beliefs or one's willingness to transfer the spiritual lessons of writing to other arenas, openness to personal growth within the writing process is a reliable way to improve one's writing. Nothing—not fancy craft techniques, not expensive MFA classes, and certainly not a high-powered publishing contract—helps us see our work with fresh eyes better than changing how those eyes see. Underneath all successful revision lies an author's open heart—a willingness to change, to be moved, to know both tears and surprise.

Revision as Incarnation

Marty, my student of many years, was born to a conservative Christian family in a virulently narrow-minded community in Wyoming. When he came out as gay, his pastor tried to reprogram him as heterosexual. Because Marty was a lawyer and a voracious reader, this involved years of in-depth theological study and long, difficult conversations. Marty was also a raging alcoholic, and one day after coming out of a bar he was targeted as gay and beaten nearly to death. I met Marty years later, after he'd sobered up, reconciled with his sexual identity, left his law practice, recovered his faith, and begun a memoir. Being bludgeoned in the head with concrete, he'd realized, was a cakewalk compared with suffering protracted theological abuse from his pastor and community. He wanted to write that story.

Never have I read a recovery memoir that was so rippingly hilarious, emotionally astute, and theologically provocative. Marty was a fantastic writer. He worked on that tome (three volumes!) for more than a decade. It was one of the most exciting projects I've ever supported.

All that while he continued conversations with his former pastor. Even as Marty came to terms with the hurt inflicted by this man, he recognized the pastor's efforts as expressions of genuine concern and love. Eventually Marty's relationship evolved into a friendship, albeit with extreme differences of opinion. Partway through our time working together, as his book grew more honest and polished, Marty realized the story he was telling would be painful to his friend. Because writing had helped Marty clarify his priorities, he eventually decided his friendship was more important than his book's publication.

I was disappointed. The world needed this book, and still does. I tried to persuade him otherwise, to no avail.

Marty kept writing, regardless. Then he was diagnosed with brain cancer. We met for coffee after he received news that his condition was terminal. I was awed by his clarity—he loved writing, he loved his project, and he was going to give a reading. A few months later, a local bookstore hosted the event; dozens of people crammed between the bookshelves and laughed and cried through Marty's stories. The evening was a living memorial service.

I'm still humbled by Marty's choice to value friendship over publication, especially since I think the pastor never knew about Marty's sacrifice. Actually, *sacrifice* is the wrong word; it was a gift, and Marty thrived as he gave it. His ability to love had grown broad and embracing, which is certainly as worthy as any literary achievement.

We writers can become single-minded: publication or bust! Our consumer culture supports this; only published work with a significant readership receives public recognition. **When writers leverage our creations in search of public affirmation, we deny our projects the benefits of full-hearted engagement.** We limit writing's potential to heal, transform, and nourish us. We also compromise our culture, which depends on literature to reconnect us with the core of our humanity, teaching us empathy and vision and ultimate meaning.

Toward what do we devote our energy? In what do we invest our love? Where do we seek meaning? These questions are ways of asking, "Where do we place our hearts?" Publication is a bridge that brings your creative work to a reader, but it is only a bridge. With the diversification of the publishing industry and the ease of online distribution, today's writers are fortunate to have many bridges to choose from. Pinning our hopes on the bridge is shortsighted. Many other outcomes for our writing are more life-giving and worthy of investment. Living a life of discovery is one, as Marty taught me. Connecting with a reader's heart is another.

Ninety-eight percent of the time I take it on faith that my writing, published or not, matters. But every once in a rare while, I get hard evidence. One evening shortly after *Swinging on the Garden Gate* was published, I had just participated in a college panel discussion about sexuality and Christianity and was heading out the door when a young woman stopped me, holding out a copy of my book for me to sign. The cover was curled, pages were dog-eared, pink highlighter marred paragraphs, and ballpoint comments filled the margins. I was aghast—had she intentionally mutilated it?

You have to understand that, as excited as I was to have Skinner House print *Swinging*, I was also disappointed, as many writers are, that the publication of my first book was not the dramatic splash I'd anticipated. For eight years I'd written with such longing, such fierce drive, and I'd assumed my ache would be satisfied by launching the story into the public realm. In the little niche *Swinging* filled (readers looking to reconcile faith with sexual identity), it did very well. I spoke on a circuit of LGBT advocacy groups, and to this day

Swinging is one of the few published books exploring the intersection of Christianity and bisexuality. But the first print run was only 750 copies. No major publication reviewed it. At the time of that panel discussion, my small endeavor seemed to be drowning in a tidal wave of books. My ache had not been assuaged. What exactly had I longed for during all those years of writing?

The young woman introduced herself as Nikki; she was a sophomore, raised Catholic, and my story had given her the courage to come out as lesbian. She thanked me profusely. I felt honored. And the state of her book now awed me: She had lived inside my story. She'd chewed it and digested it. She hadn't just read my memoir, she'd *used* it.

A few weeks later, Nikki turned up at the United Methodist Church where I was a member. She admitted to sleuthing me out. Over time, I got to know Nikki well and eventually learned that *Swinging* had awakened her call to ministry. She joined the United Methodist Church, a radical step for a born-and-bred Catholic; she attended seminary; she integrated her sexual identity with her life of faith and lived both openly.

Stories weave themselves into the fabric of our lives, irrevocably changing us. That my story did this for Nikki seems a miracle. Or perhaps the miracle is that I got to know Nikki and watch her build her own amazing story. Nikki gave me the conviction that my stories—that all our stories—can heal and transform. They can matter, to real people, in important ways. Nikki's response to *Swinging* satisfied my ache.

Art, Stephen King reminds us, is a support system for life and not the other way around. When we turn our attention toward what matters most, our creations are deeply affected—and become deeply effective.

Two of my favorite writers model these priorities beautifully. In 2014 Margaret Atwood was asked to contribute her current novel in progress to the Future Library Project, a time capsule organized by the Scottish artist Katie Paterson. One hundred authors will contribute their manuscripts, unread, unseen, to this collection, which is housed among trees that will grow to become paper for the books. They will be printed and made available in a century.

Atwood called the opportunity "delicious."

> When you write any book you do not know who's going to read it, and you do not know when they're going to read it. You don't know who they will be, you don't know their age, or gender, or nationality, or anything else about them. So books, anyway, really are like the message in the bottle.

Atwood's remarkable detachment from her work's outcome may be due to her success; perhaps she gave this project away so readily because she's gotten enough kudos from other projects. I suspect, however, that the opposite is true—her stories matter *because* she is unattached to their reception. Atwood romps in a wide field of privacy and permission.

She's not alone; when writing *Housekeeping*, Marilynne Robinson assumed she was writing an unpublishable book. "I was undistracted by other considerations than my own interest in the workings of memory and the ability of language to evoke what I 'saw' in memory." Atwood and Robinson trust profoundly the movement of their own curiosity. As they work, they jettison the idea of audience but not the craft that serves an audience. They have oriented their hearts toward what frees and enlivens them. They write for writing's sake or for the sake of their stories, then hurl their bottled messages out to sea.

In the end, aren't we writers all just writing bottled messages? Writers are an odd breed; we need paper, real or virtual, to feel fully alive and to relate constructively to the world. "I want to write," Anne Frank told her diary, "but more than that I want to bring out all kinds of things that lie buried in my heart." **Writing opens a path between the writer's stirring heart and an external, broader presence we like to personify as an audience but that may extend far beyond, to authors long dead or not yet born, to the unspoken needs of a people, to hope, to the source of life.** Call it creative process, call it meditation, call it prayer, writing is a manner of listening and conversing within and beyond ourselves.

It is, as Atwood says, "a naming of the world, a reverse incarnation: the flesh becoming word." The artistic process is inherently incarnational, as contemplation takes agency and form. Art requires the artist to contact the reality which lies beyond sensory perception, to translate this reality into accessible forms, and to willfully select and mold this material into a picture, melody, or poem. The soul I sense in my own or others' work burns with interior passion, the world's desperate needs, and a generative, transformative love. A story's soul moves the writer, which is why writing heals; it moves the reader, and it imperceptibly participates in a larger, ongoing movement shaped by and shaping history and culture. By tending the soul of a story, we tend life itself.

Literature with staying power, while grounded in the particulars of place, time, and audience, participates in conversations unlimited by place, time, and audience. Even a ten-year-old penning her first journal entry can have this experience. All writers taste it. When

I'm in the heat of writing, I'm immersed in a vast, connective sea. I know and am known. I am here, restless at my desk, and I have entirely forgotten myself. The story engaging me is only in part my invention; it's also a story we all share and are creating together. The essence of my story is already connected to others. I just have to find out how, and make that evident. I have to love it into being.

When Mark Doty was young, William Stafford read some of his poems and responded, "I have a feeling these are poems in heaven, but they're not poems on earth yet." Writers sense heaven in our drafts. We cherish it. We yearn for it. We dedicate our lives to incarnating it. The work of revision draws bits of heaven down to earth; it commingles the infinite with the finite. This divine manifestation may be our central human task. As such, the endeavor, regardless of success, is always worthwhile.

Selected Bibliography

Roseann Bane. *Around the Writer's Block: Using Brain Science to Solve Writer's Resistance.* Tarcher Perigee, 2012.

Judith Barrington. *Writing the Memoir: From Truth to Art,* 2nd ed. Eighth Mountain Press, 2002.

Charles Baxter. *The Art of Subtext: Beyond Plot.* Graywolf Press, 2007.

David Bayles and Ted Orland. *Art and Fear: Observations on the Perils (and Rewards) of Artmaking.* Image Continuum Press, 2001.

Robin Behn and Chase Twichell. *The Practice of Poetry: Writing Exercises from Poets Who Teach.* William Morrow, 1992. (See especially Susan Snively, "Waiting and Silence," and Richard Tillingast, "Household Economy, Ruthlessness, Romance, and the Art of Hospitality: Notes on Revision.")

Madison Smart Bell. *Narrative Design: Working with Imagination, Craft, and Form.* W.W. Norton & Co., 2000.

Carol Bly. *Beyond the Writer's Workshop: New Ways to Write Creative Nonfiction.* Anchor, 2001.

Robert Boice. *How Writers Journey to Comfort and Fluency: A Psychological Adventure*. Praeger, 1994.

Ray Bradbury. *Zen in the Art of Writing: Essays on Creativity*. Joshua Odell Editions, 1994.

Janet Burroway and Elizabeth Stuckey-French. *Writing Fiction: A Guide to Narrative Craft*, 9th ed. Pearson, 2014.

Louise de Salvo, *Writing as a Way of Healing: How Telling Our Stories Transforms Our Lives*. Beacon Press, 2000.

Annie Dillard. *The Writing Life*. Harper Perennial, 2013.

Carolyn Forché and Philip Gerard, eds. *Writing Creative Nonfiction*. Story Press, 2001.

E. M. Forster. *Aspects of the Novel*. Mariner Books, 1956.

John Gardner. *On Moral Fiction*. Basic Books, 1979.

Vivian Gornick. *The Situation and the Story: The Art of Personal Narrative*. Farrar, Straus & Giroux, 2002.

Emilie Griffin, ed. *A Syllable of Water: Twenty Writers of Faith Reflect on Their Art*. Paraclete Press, 2009. (See especially Diane Glancy, "After the Fire of Writing: On Revision.")

Patricia Hampl. *I Could Tell You Stories,* reprint ed. W.W. Norton & Co., 2000. (See especially "Memory and Imagination.")

Kevin Hawarth and Dinty Moore, eds. *Lit From Within: Contemporary Masters on the Art and Craft of Writing*. Ohio University Press, 2011. (See especially Robin Hemley, "Confessions of a Naval Gazer.")

Robert Henri. *The Art Spirit*. Basic Books, 2007.

Jennifer L. Holberg, ed. *Shouts and Whispers: Twenty-One Writers Speak about Their Writing and Their Faith*. Eerdmans, 2006. (See especially Katherine Paterson, "Making Meaning.")

bell hooks. *Remembered Rapture*. Holt, 1999.

Charles Johnson. *Turning the Wheel: Essays on Buddhism and Writing*. Scribner, 2007.

David Michael Kaplan. *Revision: A Creative Approach to Writing and Rewriting Fiction*. Writer's Digest Books, 2001.

Stephen King. *On Writing: A Memoir of the Craft*, 10th anniversary ed. Scribner, 2010.

Leonard Koren. *Wabi-Sabi for Artists, Designers, Poets & Philosophers*. Imperfect Publishing, 2008.

Betsy Lerner. *The Forest for the Trees: An Editor's Advice to Writers*, revised and updated. Riverhead Books, 2010.

Anne Lamott. *Bird by Bird: Some Instructions on Writing and Life*. Anchor Books, 1995.

Philip Lopate, ed. *The Art of the Personal Essay: An Anthology from the Classical Era to the Present*. Anchor Books, 1997. (See especially the Introduction.)

Dinty Moore. *Crafting the Personal Essay: A Guide for Writing and Publishing Creative Nonfiction*. Writer's Digest Books, 2010.

Flannery O'Connor. *Mystery and Manners: Occasional Prose*, selected and edited by Sally and Robert Fitzgerald. Farrar, Straus & Giroux, 1969.

Ann Patchett. *This Is the Story of a Happy Marriage,* reprint ed. Harper Perennial, 2014. (See especially "The Getaway Car.")

Francine Prose. *Reading Like a Writer: A Guide for People Who Love Books and for Those Who Want to Write Them*, reprint ed. Harper Perennial, 2007.

Rainer Maria Rilke. *Letters to a Young Poet.* Merchant Books, 2012.

Lynn Sharon Schwartz. *Ruined by Reading: A Life in Books.* Beacon Press, 1997.

Joan Silber. *The Art of Time in Fiction: As Long as It Takes.* Graywolf Press, 2009.

Daniel Slager, ed. *Views from the Loft: A Portable Writer's Workshop.* Milkweed Editions, 2010. (See especially Rick Bass, "Fiction, Nonfiction, and the Woods"; Michael Dennis Browne, "The Poem behind the Poem"; Mark Doty, "In Favor of Uncertainty"; Cheri Register, "Negotiating the Boundaries between Catharsis and Literature"; and Kim Stafford, "Open Discovery in the Art of Creative Nonfiction.")

William Stafford. *Writing the Australian Crawl: Views on the Writer's Vocation.* University of Michigan Press, 1978.

William Strunk and E. B. White. *Elements of Style,* 4th ed. Pearson, 1999.

Jennifer Traig. *The Autobiographer's Handbook.* Holt, 2008.

Peter Turchi. *Maps of the Imagination: The Writer as Cartographer.* Trinity University Press, 2007.

Brenda Ueland. *If You Want to Write: A Book about Art, Independence and Spirit.* BN Publishing, 2010.

Meredith Sue Willis. *Deep Revision: A Guide for Teachers, Students, and Other Writers.* Teachers & Writers Collaborative, 1993.

John Wilson, ed. *The Best Christian Writing 2001.* HarperOne, 2001. (See especially Alice McDermott, "Confessions of a Reluctant Catholic.")

Jay Woodruff, ed. *A Piece of Work: Five Writers Discuss Their Revisions.* University of Iowa Press, 1993.

Acknowledgments

I have not fully conveyed on these pages how much my writing is born of, developed through, and supported by others. Not all writers want or need a village to help them raise a book, but I sure do. I am profoundly grateful to my students—at the Loft Literary Center, at the Madeline Island School of the Arts, at Wisdom Ways Center for Spirituality, and in my coaching work—who have opened their drafts and hearts to me. Without their sharing, this book wouldn't be possible. I am indebted to participants in the Book Binders' Salon for their thoughtful, honest conversations about these ideas.

I remain ever grateful to my writing group: Marcia Peck, Terri Whitman, Mark Powell, and Carolyn Crooke. So much of the advice on these pages is yours! You've saved me from terrific embarrassment and been my steady source of encouragement. I wish every writer could have community like ours. Likewise, I'm indebted to Christine Sikorski for her edits; you make me seem a far better writer than I am. Thank you.

I am grateful to the Minnesota Psychoanalytic Society and Institute for awarding me the Fellowship in Applied Psychoanalysis. The psychology underpinning my work with revision was supported by Lissa Peterson and David Gordon, to whom I owe much for their time and thought.

In addition to the many authors I've cited in these pages, I'm especially thankful for those who have directly supported this project: Rosanne Bane, Cheri Register, Scott Edelstein, Beth Wright, Nancie Hughes, Mary Carroll Moore, Kate Hopper, Brenda Miller, and Monica Wesolowska. I consider myself exceedingly lucky to have the ongoing support of the Skinner House board and staff— thank you for being my bridge. I offer my deep gratitude to Mary Benard for recognizing this book's heartbeat and helping me call it forward.

Much love goes to Emily Jarrett Hughes, who participates with me daily in the Great Revision. In your honor, Emily, I wave my handkerchief.